COLLINS FOUNDATION GEOGRAPHY COURSE

GEOGRAPHY TODAY

BOOK 2

Richard Clammer
Deputy Headteacher, Brimsham Green School, Yate.
Brian Greasley
Adviser for Humanities, Sheffield LEA.
Peter McLeod
Co-ordinator of Special Educational Needs, High Green School,
Sheffield.
Richard Nicholls
formerly Head of Geography, City School, Sheffield.

Editor
Trevor Higginbottom
Chief Adviser, Barnsley LEA.

COLLINS
EDUCATIONAL

LOCATION MAP

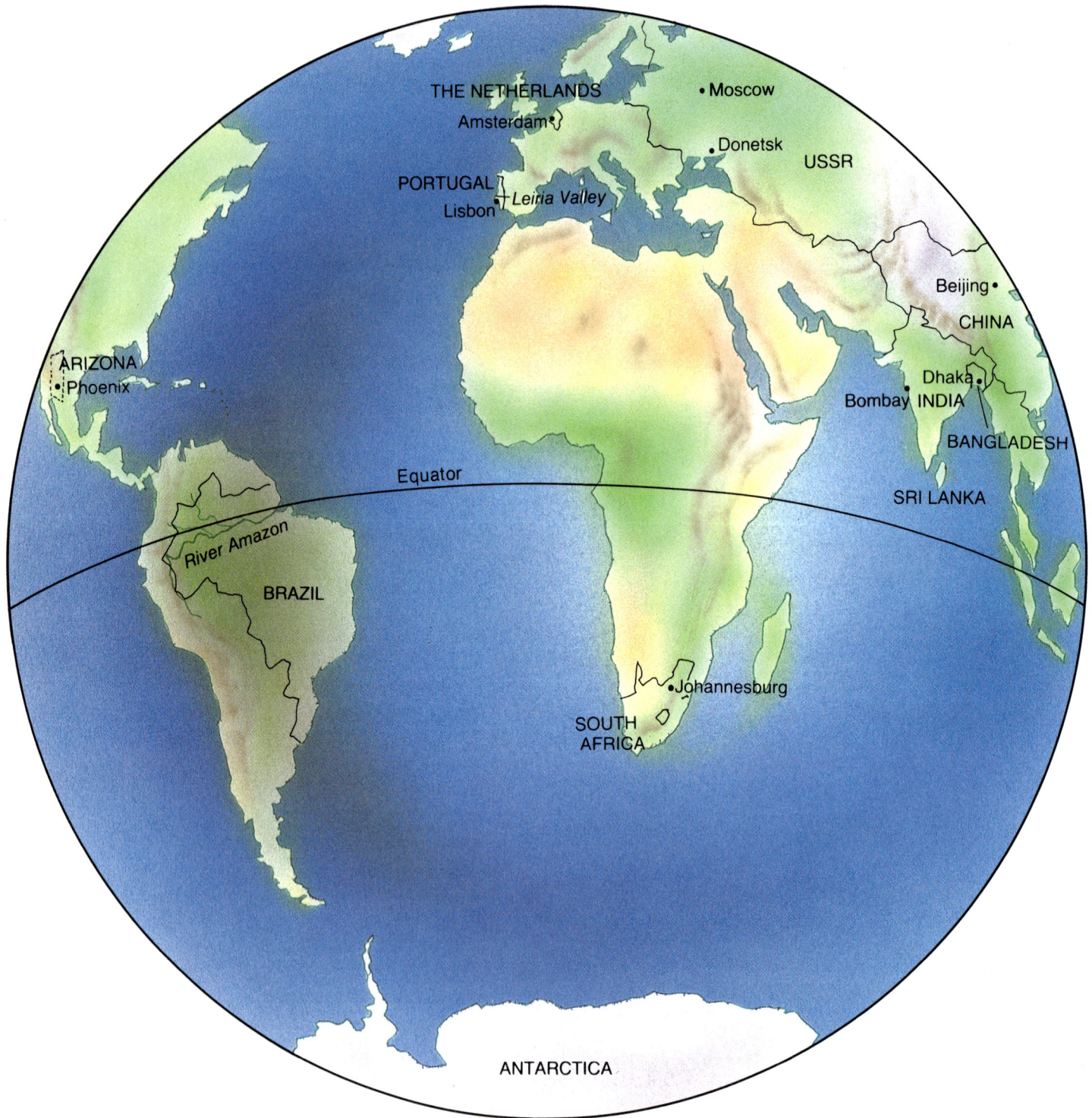

THE NETHERLANDS
• Moscow
Amsterdam
• Donetsk
USSR
PORTUGAL
+ Leiria Valley
Lisbon
Beijing •
CHINA
ARIZONA
Dhaka •
• Phoenix
Bombay INDIA
BANGLADESH
Equator
SRI LANKA
River Amazon
BRAZIL
Johannesburg
SOUTH
AFRICA

ANTARCTICA

0   2000 km
scale at Equator

CONTENTS

1 THE FUTURE OF ANTARCTICA

Until 1991 there is an Antarctic Treaty, signed by many countries, which makes sure Antarctica is only used for scientific research. What will happen after 1991? Now that minerals have been discovered, will the 'white continent' remain at peace until the 21st century?

'I have to confess an unusual addiction: I am hopelessly drawn to Antarctica'

Jan 2nd

Arrived at Rothera Station, Adelaide Island yesterday and set foot in Antarctica for the first time. We've been unloading supplies all day, no more will arrive until next year. Three ski-equipped De Havilland Twin Otter aircraft have been flying field parties out to summer camps and field huts to study GLACIERS and rocks. The accommodation is quite comfortable: I'm sharing a room with Tom who has already been out here a year. The bunk beds are OK, the food is good and the scenery superb.

Jan 3rd

We are in regular radio contact with other bases and with our Cambridge headquarters. The huts are warm and well insulated and there is plenty to do in the workshops, generator room and laboratories, as well as helping with the daily 'chores'.

No women are allowed to live at British Antarctic Survey bases, although all other countries have women working as scientists and engineers.

People who have been living here a year tell us that in winter, winds and temperatures averaging –20°C make working outside very difficult. There will only be 14 of us here during the winter out of the 65 people who passed in and out of the station during the summer.

Extracts from the diary of Jack Davis (geologist)

The Antarctic Survey base at Rothera on Adelaide Island

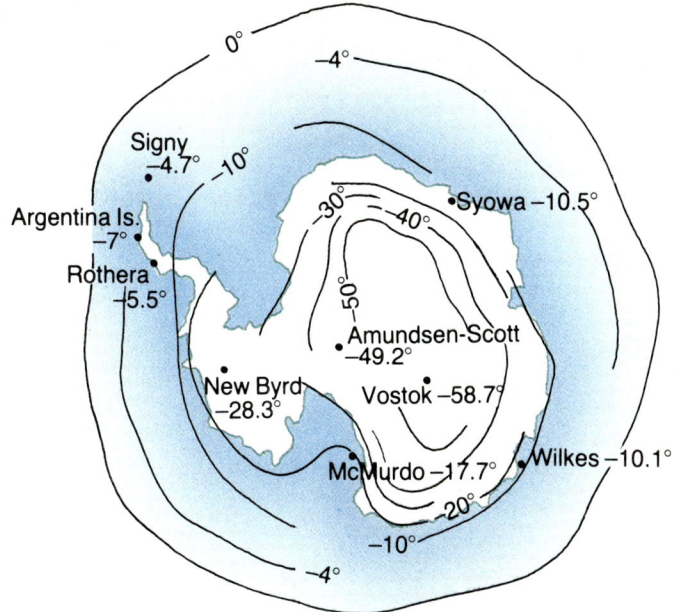

Temperatures in °C
⌒−20°⌒ Isotherms
• Stations

DEC 21st | JUNE 21st
N Arctic Circle | N Arctic Circle

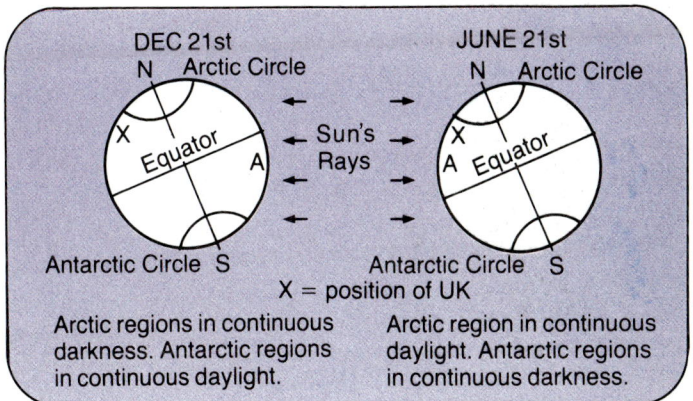

Sun's Rays

X = position of UK

Arctic regions in continuous darkness. Antarctic regions in continuous daylight. | Arctic region in continuous daylight. Antarctic regions in continuous darkness.

Jan 4th

Tom who is a METEOROLOGIST has been explaining to me why the Antarctic is so cold. Heat energy from the sun warms the earth which in turn warms air above it. Tom drew the diagram on the right, to show that even on midsummer's day (Dec 21st) the sun's rays do not reach the earth's suface directly as at A, but at an angle. This means that the heating effect is much less in Antarctica than at A.

Also there is often cloud cover in Antarctica so much of the sun's heat energy never reaches the ground. Some 50% to 60% of the energy which does reach the surface is reflected by the great white sheet of ice.

Antarctica is colder than the Arctic because it is much higher. In fact it is the world's highest CONTINENT averaging over 2 000 metres in height. The world's lowest temperatures are experienced in the Antarctic. At the Soviet station of Vostok, over 3 000 metres above sea level, −88°C has been recorded.

Jan 5th

Went sunbathing today! In the short Antarctic summer it is possible to sunbathe as long as there is no wind. It is the wind which makes the Antarctic feel so cold. No rain falls on the ice sheet. The snow fall is light and consists of fine grains, and only amounts to some 50 mm per year. The air is dry. But the wind blowing outwards from the centre of the continent can make conditions very difficult.

I was reading 'Home of the Blizzard' by Sir Douglas Mawson last night. He wrote about some of the conditions we may have here: 'Picture a DRIFT so dense that daylight comes through dully, even though the sun shines in a cloudless sky; the drift is hurled, screaming through space at a hundred miles an hour.'

❶ Imagine that you are the person in the picture opposite.
ⓐ List ten words which describe your thoughts and feelings as you look across Antarctica. Then write three or four sentences using your words.
ⓑ Write a paragraph for your diary describing:
(i) Rothera Station,
(ii) the weather in Antarctica.

❷ ⓐ On a copy of the map of MEAN ANNUAL SURFACE TEMPERATURES at the top of the page complete the temperature lines.
ⓑ What pattern is shown by the lines?
ⓒ Complete the sentence: 'As one goes closer to the centre of Antarctica and further from the sea the temperature _____ .

❸ Look at Tom's diagram and the diary extract for Jan 4th. Copy and complete these sentences: 'When it is winter in Great Britain it is _____ in Antarctica. When it is winter in Antarctica it is _____ in Great Britain.'

3

The great white continent

Jan 18th
Today I developed and printed the photographs I took on my way here of my first iceberg – it was a tabular iceberg with a flat top and it was about 5 kilometres long and 30 metres high. It was very white and beautiful. The captain kept our ship well clear of the iceberg as about four-fifths of all icebergs are underwater. Icebergs are large sections of the ice shelf which break off and float away. I also took photographs of large areas of sea ice, known as 'pack ice'. This ice drifts with the aid of winds and sea currents.

A tabular iceberg in Antarctica. Icebergs can be over 150 kilometres in length and 30 metres in height above sea level.

Measuring the speed of the movement of a glacier in Antarctica.

Jan 25th
This morning I spoke on the radio telephone to Peter about a joint field trip. He is a GEOLOGIST at Halley station. The station is on the Brunt Ice Shelf which is part of the great ICE SHEET floating out onto the sea. Snow has piled up slowly over Antarctica for so many years that it now covers 95% of the continent. The ice sheet is so heavy that much of the underlying land has been pressed below sea level. The ice is over 1 000 metres thick on average and it moves outwards towards the coast. As it moves through the mountains it forms glaciers. It has been estimated that it would take a particle of ice 100 000 years to move from the South Pole to the sea. Near the sea the ice is thinner and moving at some 400 metres a year down the glaciers to the coast.

Cross section of Antarctica showing underlying land surface

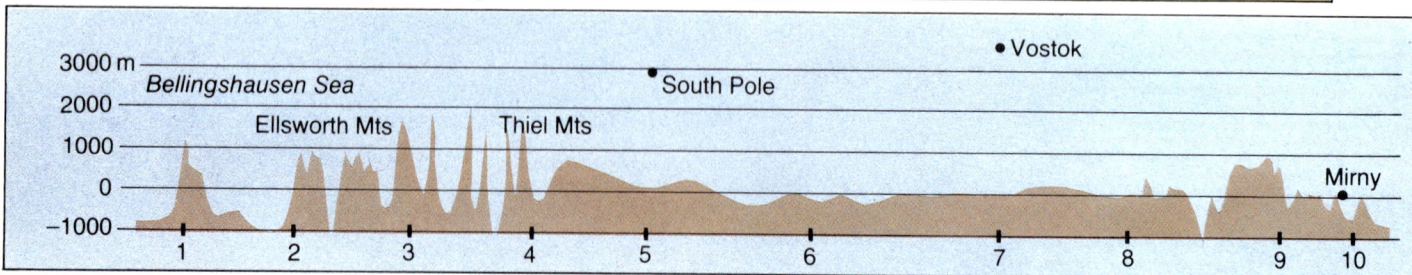

Height of ice sheet above sea level in metres

Point	Height (metres)	Point	Height (metres)
1	1 000	6	3 100
2	1 250	7	3 300
3	1 250	8	3 100
4	1 500	9	2 200
5	2 900	10	0

❶ Why do you think the flat topped icebergs are called tabular icebergs? (Hint: what does the word tabular sound like?)

❷ If the iceberg is 30 metres high, how deep underwater will the rest of it be? (Hint: 30 metres is one fifth.)

❸ ⓐ On a copy of the cross section mark on the depth of the ice at points 1–10 from the table. Join the points with a smoothly curving line.
ⓑ Look at your cross-section:
(i) How deep is the ice at the South Pole?
(ii) How deep is the ice at Vostok station?

Map showing the movement of the continents

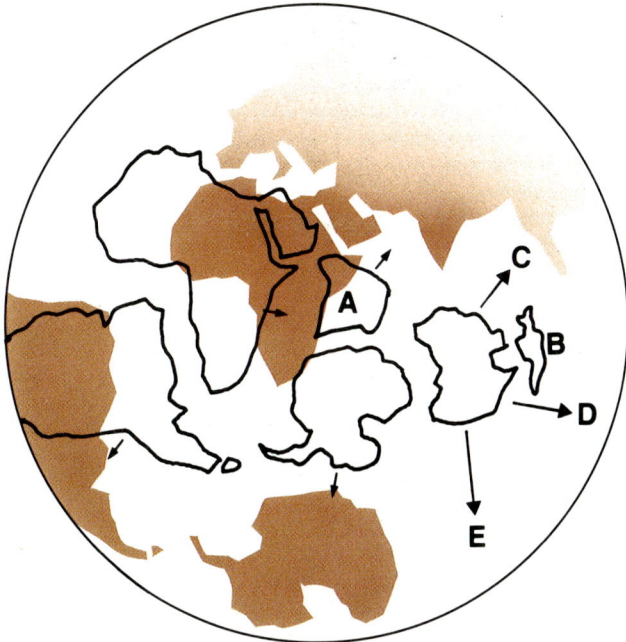

(The outlines show the position 100 million years ago, the shaded areas show their position today)

February 10th
Field study at last! We were taken by aircraft to the Transantarctic mountains. Being a GEOLOGIST I found them very interesting. COAL SEAMS were easy to see. The southern continents were once one big continent called Gondwanaland which drifted apart about 140 million years ago. We've even found the FOSSIL remains of a dinosaur known as a Lystrosaurus in Beachmore glacier. Similar fossils are well known in southern Africa.

I was lucky today as I found some fossil ferns. When I was telling John, another geologist, working nearby, he showed me *trilobite* fossils he had found. They are small sea shellfish with a flattened body which lived 600 million years ago. About 172 million years ago volcanic eruptions created great areas of volcanic rock in the Pensacola Mountains. Mount Erebus, on Ross Island, is still an active volcano today.

Mount Erebus, Ross Island

Ferns

Trilobite – Ehmania

❹ Look at the map at the top of the page, showing the movement of the continents. Use an atlas and:
ⓐ Name land areas **A** and **B**.
ⓑ Did Australia move in direction C, D, or E on the map?

❺ *What do the fossils tell us about conditions in Antarctica in the past?*

The world's greatest science park?

A Studying plant life
Plants grow in areas where the snow melts in the short summer. Scientists are studying how the plants survive in these difficult conditions and how environmental changes might affect their growth.

B Looking at rock formations
A great deal of research is being done into the rocks of Antarctica and the ocean around the continent. Scientists are also looking for places where minerals and other raw materials could be mined.

C Animal research
Scientists are studying the lives of the many creatures which live in and around the Antarctic.

During the two-month South Polar summer (October to November) more than 3 000 specialists from 20 different nations spread out across the Antarctic ice. Why?

F Looking at the weather
Antarctica is a good place for conducting experiments into the world's weather. Scientists are already carrying out research into the OZONE LAYER of the upper atmosphere.

D Ice-sheet air pollution
Evidence of all the air pollution which has ever been produced is locked up in the glaciers and ice sheets. Already, evidence goes back to the time Julius Caesar invaded Great Britain (55 BC).

E Understanding the earth's magnetic field
Ultra violet radiation and electrically charged particles from the sun affect the earth's magnetic field This causes problems for ships and aircraft which rely on sensitive navigating equipment to guide them. Antarctica is an ideal place to find out more.

GAS AND OIL
Several countries and companies are interested in test drilling in areas where geologists have discovered rock layers where oil and gas may be found.

COPPER AND MOLYBDENUM
These metals and others are found in the Antarctic Peninsula (a continuation of the Andes) but not in quantities large enough to mine.

ICEBERGS
Several countries have shown interest in the possibility of floating icebergs to desert areas to supply fresh water.

URANIUM
Small amounts of uranium are found in rocks similar to those in South Africa.

FISHING
Whale and seal catches are now limited by international law. Krill, a high PROTEIN shrimp-like creature provides a rich source of food. Over-fishing is already causing their numbers to fall.

IRON
High grade iron-ore deposits are found in layers up to 25 metres thick.

COAL
Good quality coal found in seams 3 metres thick and 2 kilometres long.

Orange Basin
B
Outemgua Basin
E
0°
South Shetland Is.
Weddel Sea
A
Magallanes Basin oil field
Bellingshausen Sea
90°E
TRANSANTARCTIC MTS
South Pole
90°W
Amundsen Sea
Ross Sea
SOUTHERN OCEAN
60°S Latitude
Gippsland Basin
Kingfisher Barracoota Halibut oil fields
D
180°
C
Maui oil field

Key

- - - - Edge of Ice Shelf

■ Exposed rock

⊙ Production oil fields

▨ Active exploration area

▨ Potenial exploration area

0   2000
km

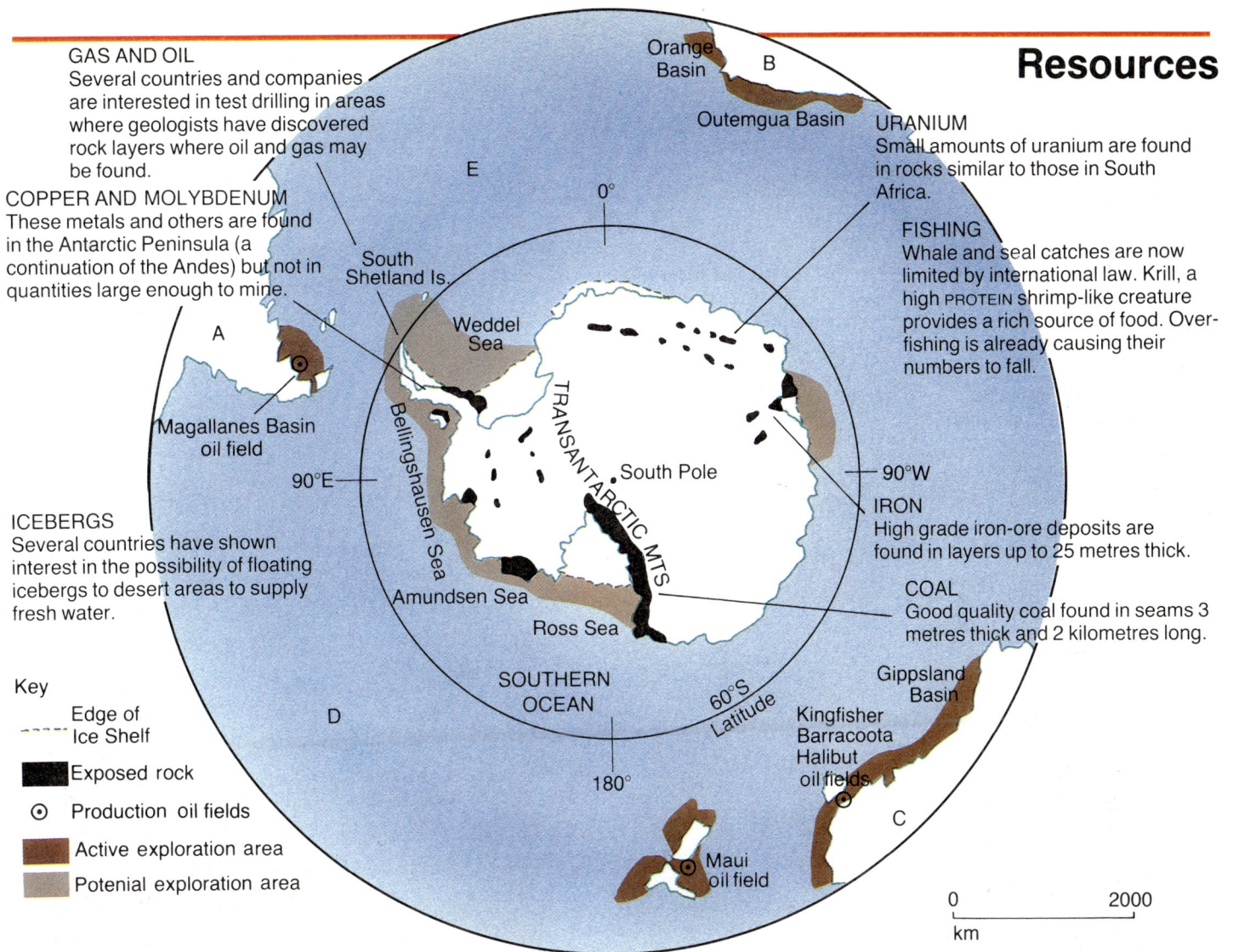

August 3rd
I spent the morning talking with other geologists about the RESOURCES of Antarctica. Apart from the ice and fishing, a large number of MINERALS have been found. The map above shows the main deposits.

Gas and oil are attracting a lot of attention. However, the technology to deal with the hazards of pack ice which can crush a ship, long storms and the ever present icebergs does not yet exist and would be very expensive to develop.

As for mining on land, the difficulties are enormous. Only 5% of Antarctica is ice free and mining under great thicknesses of ice is only just being investigated. The problems of moving the ore to the coast, of building a port, of providing supplies and of ships moving in icy waters are obvious. The company would also be working in some of the most difficult weather conditions in the world.

❶ Look at the pictures of scientists working in Antarctica on the opposite page.
 Match the letters A–F to the correct name of the scientist from the list below.
  A glaciologist – studies glaciers and ice
  A geologist – studies rocks
  A zoologist – studies animals
  A meteorologist – studies the weather
  A physicist – studies the forces of nature
  A biologist – studies plants and small creatures

❷ Look at the map above. Use your atlas to help you name the following:
 ⓐ the continents labelled A, B and C;
 ⓑ the oceans labelled D and E.

❸ *Draw a diagram to show how you might be able to move a large iceberg from Antarctica to a desert country to be used as a source of fresh water. (You would not be able to tow it from the front because it would nose dive.)*

❹ *Write down a list or draw a diagram to show what you would need to start a mining operation in Antarctica.*

Planning for the future

August 10th

Tom and I were late going to sleep last night. We were talking about what would happen to the Antarctic if companies come here to mine the minerals.

An oil spill from drilling operations would be difficult to clean up in Antarctic ice conditions. If anything went wrong, like an oil well catching fire, it would take over a year just to get the men and equipment together to put it out. Tom was telling me that it has already taken over a year to put out an oil fire in the Arctic.

Bases for mining operations would be limited to the smooth ice-free coasts, and it's just on these few areas that the richest flowers and animal life are to be found: they would be destroyed. The operations would look ugly here and the dirt, dust and smoke would spoil the landscape.

Another point is how do you get rid of waste when things rot very slowly? Some tinned food 60 years old has been found in good condition in the Antarctic deep freeze!

The problem with all this is we don't know enough. Perhaps we should find out more before we start.

Rear Admiral Byrd, who led the United States Antarctic Expedition in 1935, revisits his old hut in 1947. He is smoking the tobacco which he left there twelve years before.

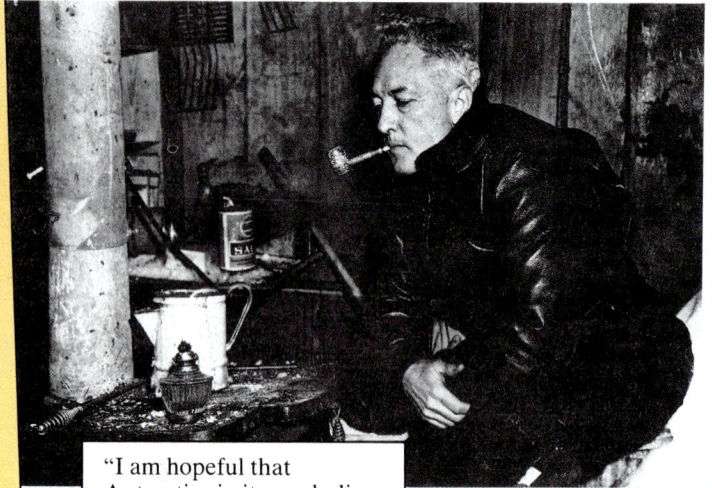

"I am hopeful that Antarctica in its symbolic robe of white will shine forth as a continent of peace, as nations working together there in the cause of science set an example of international co-operation."

Inscription on the statue to Rear Admiral Richard Byrd

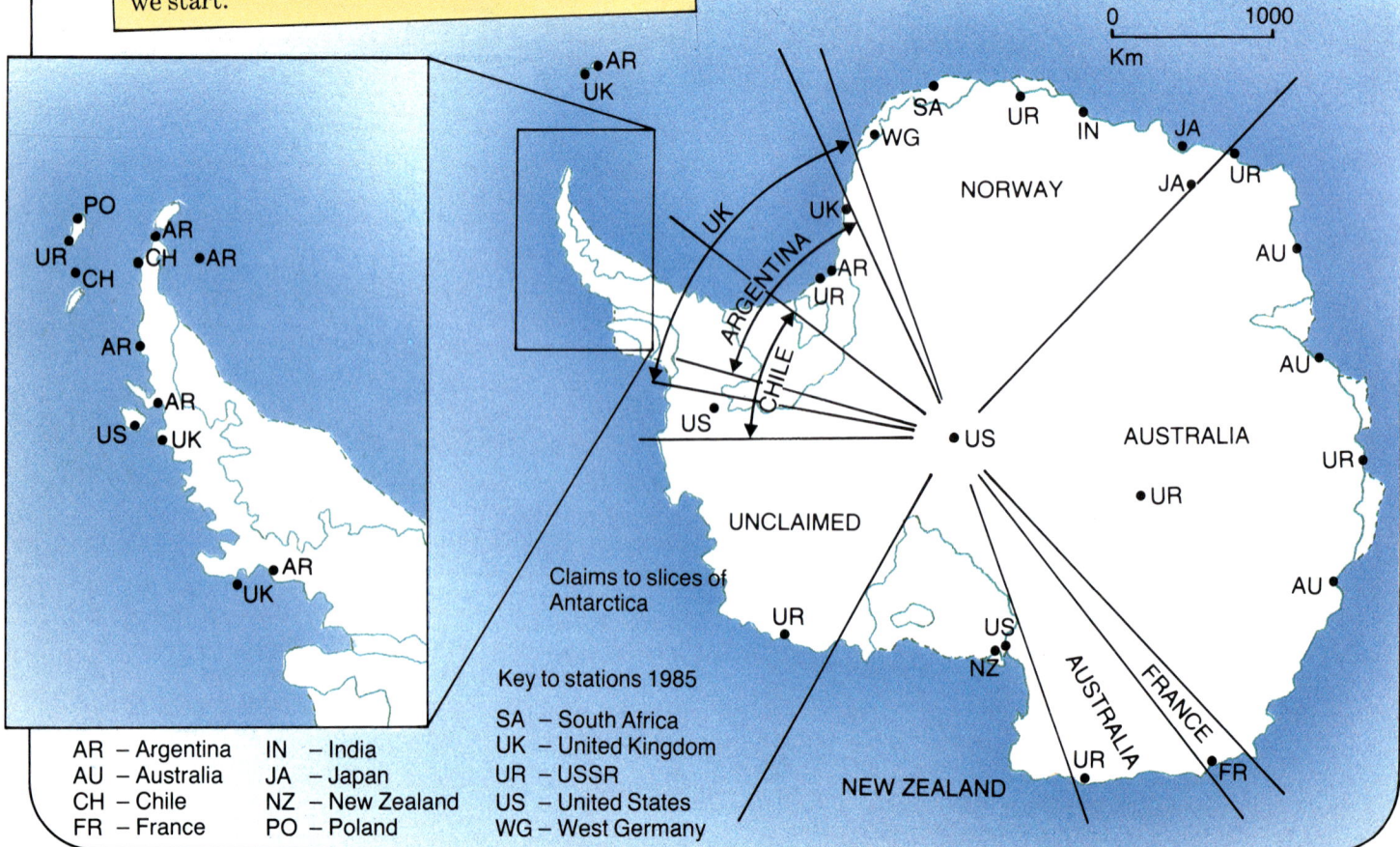

Claims to slices of Antarctica

Key to stations 1985

AR – Argentina	IN – India
AU – Australia	JA – Japan
CH – Chile	NZ – New Zealand
FR – France	PO – Poland
	SA – South Africa
	UK – United Kingdom
	UR – USSR
	US – United States
	WG – West Germany

December 30th

It is nearly a year since I first came to Antarctica. I went to the McMurdo Sound United States base today and saw the statue to Admiral Byrd who established the first US station here.

The inscription set Tom and me thinking. In 1959 the Antarctic Treaty was signed. There are now 32 members. The Treaty stated that the Antarctic should be used for peaceful and scientific purposes and all claims to govern territory were suspended. It worked!

In 1991 the Treaty comes to an end. Already people are wondering what will happen, especially if minerals are found in large quantities. The Greenpeace organisation is already campaigning for Antarctica to become a World National Park.

The discussion about what should happen went on all the way back to Rothera. This evening we all sat round the dining table trying to decide what would be the best solution.

After 1991 Antarctica could be:

A A World Park

All mineral exploration and mining would be banned, permanently or at least until a lot more research had been done so that minerals could be obtained without environmental damage.

Action: Antarctic Treaty members declare the area a World Park and bring the agreement to the United Nations for the global community to accept.

B Governed by a group of countries

Antarctica would be governed jointly by the members of the Antarctic Treaty.

Action: Antarctic Treaty replaced by an agreement between the members to govern the area, joint decisions would be taken about exploration and mining.

C Governed globally

All nations of the world would share in making decisions about Antarctica.

Action: Antarctic Treaty replaced by new treaty and all nations of the world become involved in governing the continent.

> You would never get agreement between all nations if really rich minerals were discovered.

> Surely people realize we can't all have a share so why not save Antarctica for everyone – too much exploitation would destroy it.

> The Old Treaty must be replaced but it will be difficult as so many nations want a part of Antarctica. I think control should stay with the present Treaty members as they are the only ones who really know the area.

> A World Park is the only solution which would protect the environment for ever.

> We have to decide something before 1991 or there will be a mad scramble to take over Antarctica. This could even lead to war.

❶ Look at the map 'Claims to slices of Antarctica' on the opposite page.
ⓐ List all the countries that have a piece of Antarctica. Then, beside each country, note down the number of experimental stations they have.
ⓑ Which three countries have the most stations?

❷ *Choose four countries and try to decide why they, in particular, have claimed a part of Antarctica.*

❸ Divide into groups of four or five, and decide which of the three possible solutions to the future of Antarctica you feel would be the best.

Write out your solution, with the reasons for your choice, on a large sheet of paper. Report your decision and the reasons to the rest of the class. Discuss the solutions as a class group.

Why not investigate?

Research into the story of one of the great Antarctic expeditions, like those of Scott, Shackleton, Amundsen or Fuchs.

2 SPARE THOSE TREES

The world's forests are being destroyed at an alarming rate. How is this happening? Why is CONSERVATION needed urgently?

Brazil and its neighbouring countries

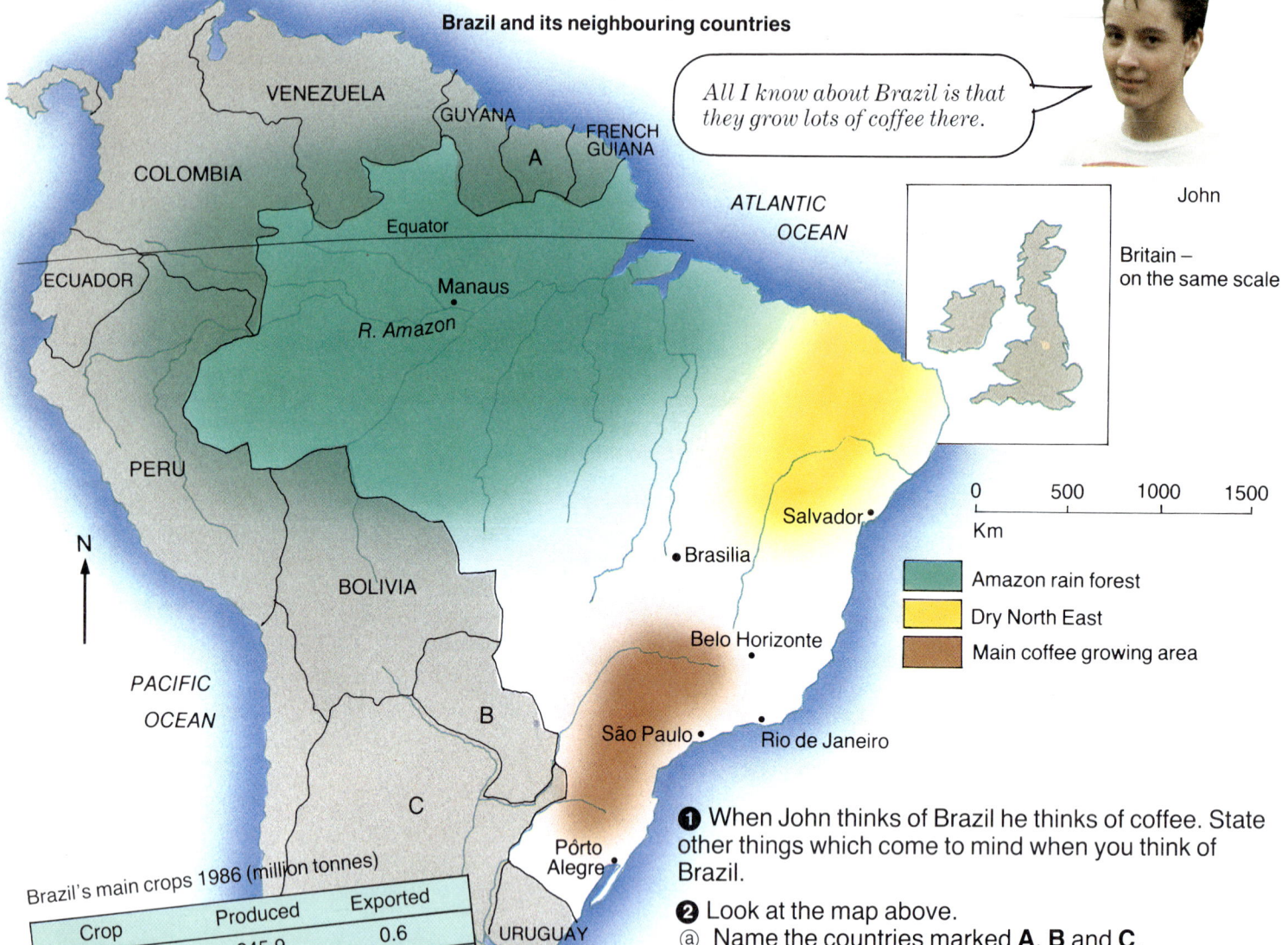

> *All I know about Brazil is that they grow lots of coffee there.*

John

Britain – on the same scale

VENEZUELA
GUYANA
FRENCH GUIANA
A
COLOMBIA
Equator
ECUADOR
Manaus
R. Amazon
ATLANTIC OCEAN
PERU
N
BOLIVIA
Salvador
Brasilia
PACIFIC OCEAN
Belo Horizonte
B
São Paulo
Rio de Janeiro
C
Pôrto Alegre
URUGUAY

0	500	1000	1500

Km

- Amazon rain forest
- Dry North East
- Main coffee growing area

Brazil's main crops 1986 (million tonnes)

Crop	Produced	Exported
Sugar cane	245.9	0.6
Maize	22.0	—
Soya beans	18.2	—
Rice	9.0	—
Coffee	3.7	2.5
Cotton	1.8	0.4

Brazils land use 1986

Land use	Percentage of Brazil's area
Forest	60
Grass	13
Arable (crops)	4
Other uses (cities, roads, waste, etc)	23

❶ When John thinks of Brazil he thinks of coffee. State other things which come to mind when you think of Brazil.

❷ Look at the map above.
ⓐ Name the countries marked **A**, **B** and **C**.
ⓑ What is the distance from the border with Uruguay in the south of Brazil to the border of French Guiana in the north?
ⓒ Copy and complete the following:

The River Amazon starts in the Andes Mountains in _____ . After it enters Brazil it flows in a _____ direction towards the _____ Ocean. From its source to its mouth it flows about _____ kilometres.

❸ Study the table of Brazil's main crops on the left.
ⓐ Was John right to think of coffee as an important Brazilian crop? Explain your answer (make sure you look at the amount of coffee exported).
ⓑ Why do you think rice and maize are not exported?

❹ Using the table on the left, draw a divided bar graph to show land use in Brazil. Label it.

The rain forest

ADVENTURE TOURS – THE AMAZON
THE CLIMATE IN MANAUS

Day 3
After a night at the Tropical Hotel, leave at 6 am for an unforgettable journey into the amazingly beautiful Amazon forest. Board a speedy boat for a 1½ hour journey to the Amazon Lodge. Make an expedition to the crocodile lagoon where local people catch crocodiles with their bare hands.

Day 4
Wake before dawn and take a boat into the forest to see the forest dwellers come to life. Thousands of exotic and colourful birds leave their roosts and fish leap from the quiet waters. Spend the morning exploring the incredible plant and animal life of the forest. The Amazon area contains one-third of the world's trees. Five hundred types of tree have been found within a small area and some of them are very rare. Catch one of the 1 500 species of edible fish that live in the Amazon and its tributaries.

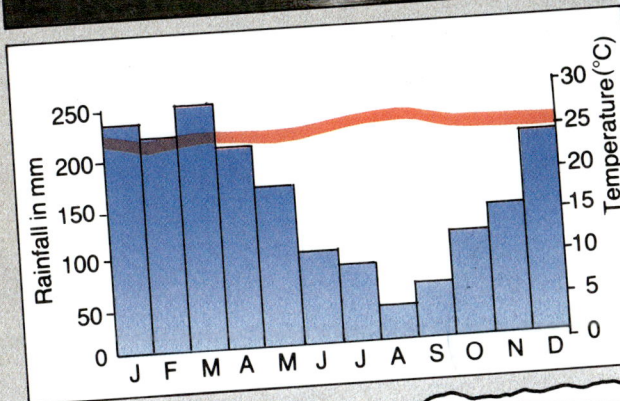

The Tropical Hotel,
Manaus,
August 15th

Dear Kate and Brian,

We're in Manaus now, by the Amazon River right in the heart of the forest. Our hotel is very comfortable and modern in the centre of a large and flourishing town. There are some lovely old buildings here too.

It is so hot, all day and every day. Just walking around makes your clothes stick to you. During the afternoon the clouds build up until about 4 o'clock when it rains. Not just ordinary rain but a storm with thunder and lightning. It doesn't last long, though. Our guide says it's like this all the year and that's why there's such dense forest here.

We went into the forest yesterday. It was very lovely but quite eerie. As we entered the forest, the sun disappeared. But it was easier to walk through than I had imagined. There was little undergrowth – just tall trees – with the tallest having wide buttress roots to keep them upright. There were thick lianas like huge ropes hanging from the branches. The silence was quite frightening though. Apart from a few birds screeching, all you could hear was our party slapping at mosquitoes. And this forest is three times the size of France …

With best wishes,

Helen

5 Study the climate graph above.
ⓐ What is the average temperature in most months?
ⓑ What is the average rainfall in March and in October?

6 From the letter on the left, describe the main features of the weather each day.

7 Suggest two reasons why the letter writer might have chosen to go to the Manaus area in August.

8 How does the photograph above help to explain why the sun disappears as you enter the forest?

9 From the statements below, write down those you think are correct.
ⓐ It is easy to walk through the Amazon forest because there is no undergrowth.
ⓑ The quickest way to get through the forest is to swing on lianas.
ⓒ The forest is quiet and eerie.
ⓓ There are many insects which can cause discomfort.

10 Would you like to visit the Amazon? Work in pairs. Suggest reasons for and against going there for a holiday.

The forest is home for some people

Nambiquara boys fishing

It must be great to live in a place like this, with all those animals and birds.

The Nambiquara people are one of many groups who live in the Amazon forest. Their way of life makes it possible for them to live in an area where we would find it hard to survive.

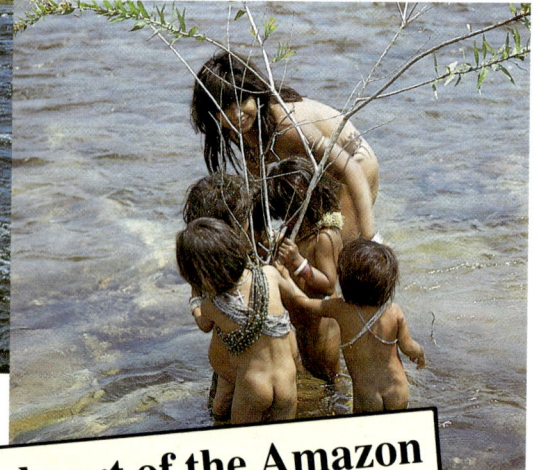

Force of rain broken by canopy of trees

Leaves fall and rot down to make humus

Shallow roots to get nourishment from humus

Rich layer of humus

INFERTILE SOIL

A Trees provide their own plant food

Nothing to stop heavy rain beating on the ground

Trees cut down and burnt

Humus layer quickly washed away

INFERTILE SOIL

B When the trees go the rich humus layer does not last for long

In the heart of the Amazon

I visited a small settlement of palm-thatched huts by the river. A woman was pounding MANIOC roots to make flour. She said, 'Manioc is a type of bush but only the root is eaten. Some kinds of manioc contain a poisonous juice. One way to make the manioc root edible is to peel it, soak it in water, pound it and put it into a press, sift it and finally heat it.'

I asked the woman where the manioc grew. She showed me a track through the forest to a clearing a kilometre away. There, her husband was weeding with a large knife (machete). A spade or plough would not have been suitable for this kind of ground. Large charred tree-trunks lay on the floor of the clearing which was not very fertile any more.

'The soil is exhausted after two or three years', she said. 'Then we have to make a new clearing.' With about two hectares a couple and their family can live.

She described the traditional way of making a clearing. 'The undergrowth and lianas are hacked down. The trees are cut down and, when it is dry enough, everything in set on fire. The ashes help to fertilise the soil.'

As well as manioc, rice and beans were grown in the clearing. To add to the family diet, the husband hunted deer and wild pig. He also caught fish.

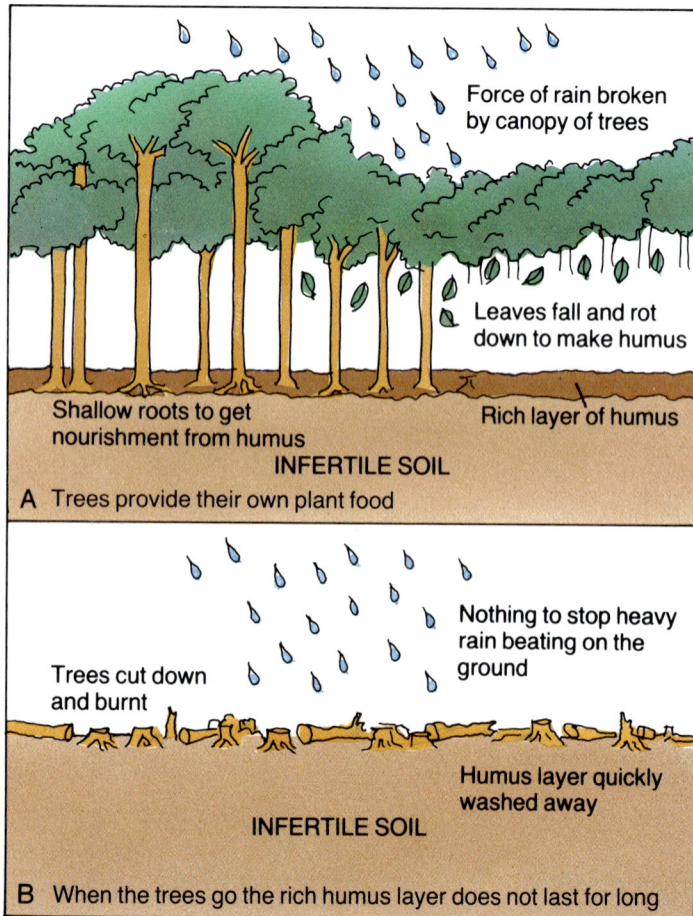

A part of the Amazon forest

Native village

Forest clearing

0 1 2 3 4
Km

A

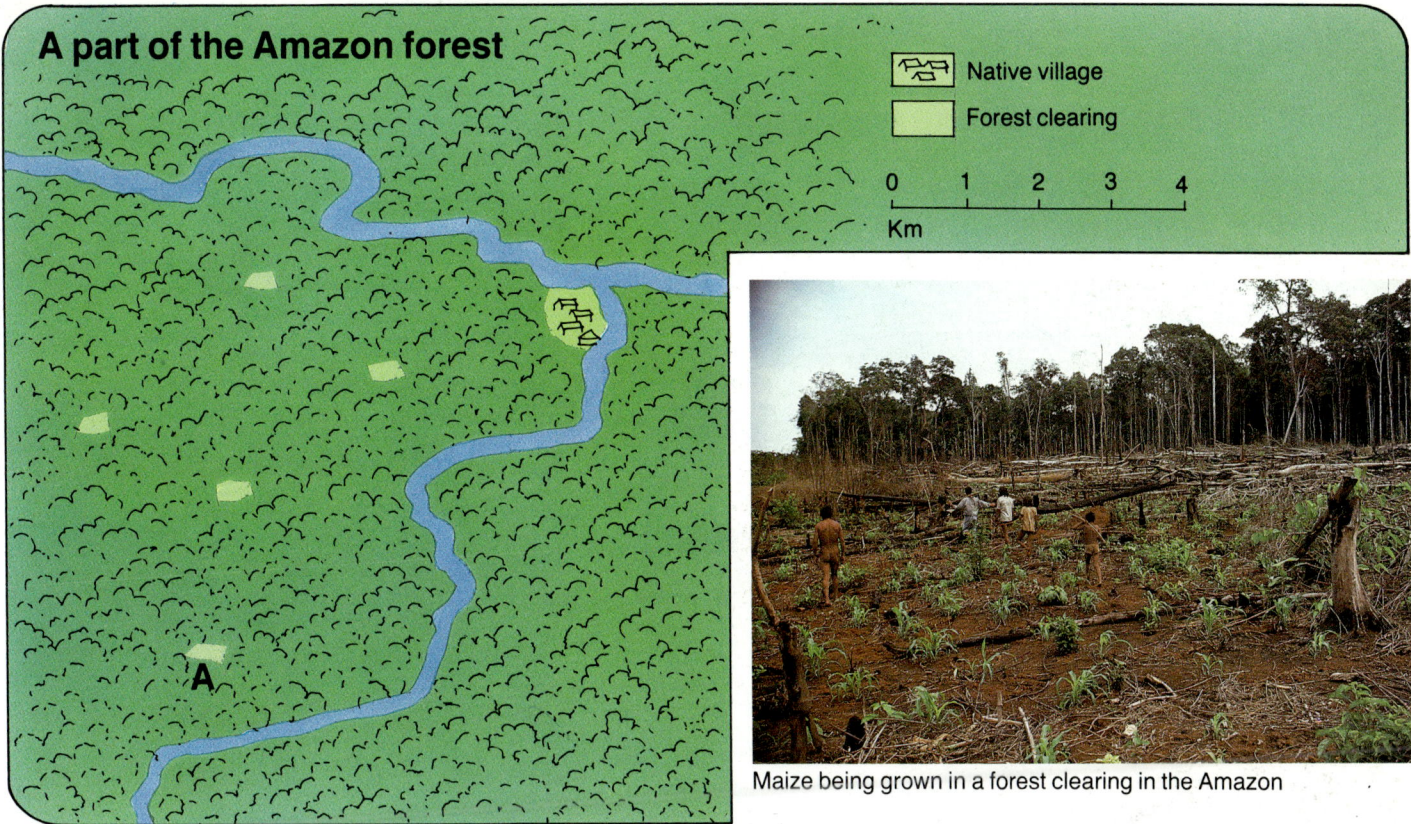

Maize being grown in a forest clearing in the Amazon

❶ Study the diagrams **A** and **B** on the opposite page. Then explain:
ⓐ how a thick forest is able to grow in infertile soil;
ⓑ the effect of cutting down trees.

❷ Write a few sentences to describe the scene in the photograph above.

❸ Make a large copy of the diagram below. Complete it to show how the Nambiquara people cultivate land in the forest. You will need to refer to the article 'In the heart of the Amazon'.

START
A new clearing is made by
_____

Seeds are sown on the cleared land

Weeding _____
_____
_____

Crops of _____
_____
are harvested 3-4 months later

The soil _____
_____
_____

❹ Why do you think this method of farming is called shifting cultivation?

❺ ⓐ What do you think will happen to a clearing when it has been abandoned?
ⓑ Why do you think the land can be cultivated again after 20 to 30 years?

❻ Study the map of 'A part of the Amazon forest'.
ⓐ How many clearings are used to grow food for people in the village?
ⓑ How far is the furthest clearing from the village?
ⓒ What would be the easier way to reach the clearing marked **A**?
ⓓ State two advantages and one possible disadvantage of building the village near a river.

❼ Why do you think the Nambiquara people do not need to have contact with the world outside the forest? Give your reasons.

❽ ⓐ *Why can shifting cultivation only support a small number of people?*
ⓑ *What would happen if a large number of people, in a small area of forest, tried to live by shifting cultivation?*

❾ *Do you think the Brazilian government should allow native villages to be visited by tourist groups? Give your reasons.*

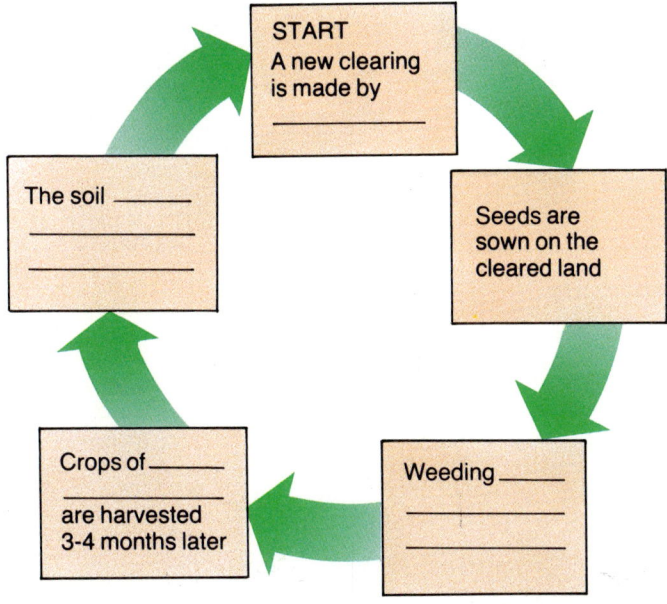

13

Exploiting the forest land

The Brazilian Military Government in the 1970s had great plans for the Amazon forest area.

Is there a more profitable way of using the forest than shifting cultivation? — John

THE DROUGHT IN THE NORTH-EAST OF THE COUNTRY IS CAUSING PROBLEMS. WE COULD OFFER THE PEASANTS LAND IN THE AMAZON FOREST AREA.

THE PEASANTS WILL NOT COME CROWDING INTO THE CITIES WHERE THERE ARE ALREADY SHORTAGES OF HOMES AND WORK.

THE NEW SETTLERS WILL PROVIDE MAIZE, RICE AND BEANS FOR THE PEOPLE IN THE CITIES. AND GROW COFFEE, COTTON AND ORANGES AND OTHER CROPS TO SELL ABROAD.

LET US ENCOURAGE FOREIGN FIRMS TO HELP US MAKE THE AMAZON FOREST AREA A PROSPEROUS PART OF THE COUNTRY.

IT WOULD BE USEFUL TO BUILD NEW ROADS THROUGH THE FOREST. THEN WE COULD MOVE WORKERS AND MACHINERY INTO THE AREA AND GET RAW MATERIALS OUT. ALSO WE COULD MOVE TROOPS MORE EASILY IF A NEIGHBOURING COUNTRY ATTACKED US.

As a result the directors of a large foreign car company make plans.

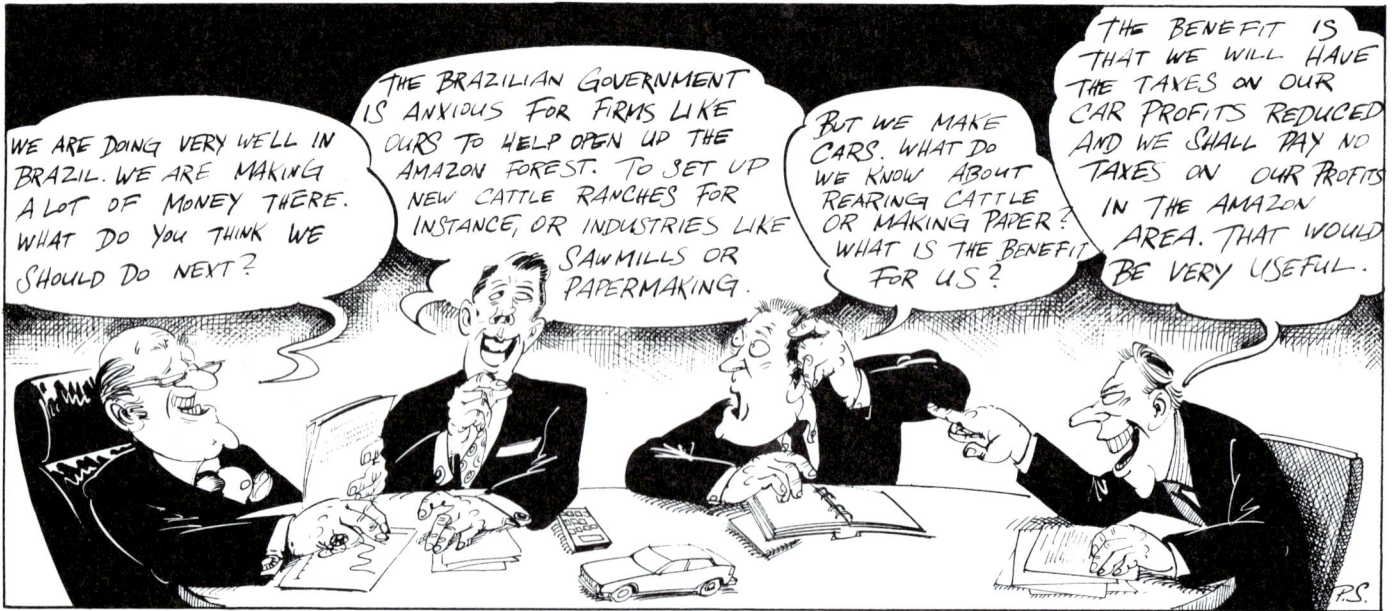

WE ARE DOING VERY WELL IN BRAZIL. WE ARE MAKING A LOT OF MONEY THERE. WHAT DO YOU THINK WE SHOULD DO NEXT?

THE BRAZILIAN GOVERNMENT IS ANXIOUS FOR FIRMS LIKE OURS TO HELP OPEN UP THE AMAZON FOREST. TO SET UP NEW CATTLE RANCHES FOR INSTANCE, OR INDUSTRIES LIKE SAWMILLS OR PAPERMAKING.

BUT WE MAKE CARS. WHAT DO WE KNOW ABOUT REARING CATTLE OR MAKING PAPER? WHAT IS THE BENEFIT FOR US?

THE BENEFIT IS THAT WE WILL HAVE THE TAXES ON OUR CAR PROFITS REDUCED AND WE SHALL PAY NO TAXES ON OUR PROFITS IN THE AMAZON AREA. THAT WOULD BE VERY USEFUL.

❶ Suggest four reasons why the Brazilian Government wanted to EXPLOIT the Amazon forest?

❷ What did the government want foreign firms to do?

❸ How did the government encourage the foreign firms to help to exploit the forest area?

❹ Draw a pie chart to illustrate the table on the right.

Reasons for cutting down the Amazon forest	
	Percentage of area felled
Ranching	38%
Crops	31%
Roads	27%
Other (e.g. mining)	4%

14

The 400 million-dollar plan

Selected farmers, mainly from the North-east, are given 100 hectare plots each with a 500 metre frontage along a main road. These farmers are not used to the soil and weather conditions in the area. At 100 kilometre intervals there is an 'agrovilas'. This is a town containing shops, a school, a health centre and some industry. About 56 million hectares have been taken up in this way since 1964.

Logging companies cut hardwoods in the Amazon forest for sawn timber, plywood and veneers (which are used for panelling). Also the Japanese have discovered how to make pulp and paper from hardwoods.

Nearly 20% of Brazil's petrol needs have been replaced by alcohol fuel. The alcohol is distilled from sugar cane which can be grown on land cleared of forest.

An Italian gas company has carved out a ranch of 600 600 hectares from which beef is exported. Only a few charred trunks remain of the forest.

Sao Luis

— Major highways

▼ Major dams

⬟ Mineral deposits

Thousands of kilometres of highway have been built through the forest.

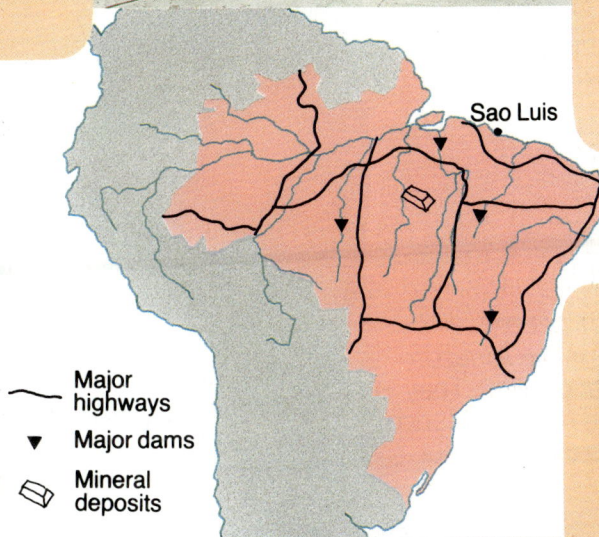

A new port, Sao Luis, has been built to export metal ores. An electric railway, 940 kilometres long, connects the mines of the Carajas Iron Ore Project with the port.

A new dam has been built at Tucurui to provide power for the railway. The electricity is also used to process bauxite which is used to make aluminium.

Huge deposits of minerals have been discovered: 18 000 million tonnes of iron ore and 70 million tonnes of bauxite.

❺ Name six ways in which the forest area is being used to create wealth for Brazil and employment for its people.

❻ Why do you think the first move was to build highways through the forest?

❼ What is done to encourage small farmers to move into the area?

❽ Why is the growth of sugar cane encouraged?

❾ ⓐ Which developments are likely to be carried out by foreign firms?
ⓑ What are the advantages to Brazil of foreign firms operating in the Amazon forest?

❿ What do you think the effect of developing the Amazon rain forest will be on people like the Nambiquara people who have been practising shifting cultivation?

Why conserve the rain forests?

Do only a few people who are already rich benefit from the exploitation of the rain forests? If the rain forests are destroyed, do we all stand to lose?

People like the Nambiquara live in the rain forest. They cannot stand up to those who are invading the forest and threatening them and their way of life. They have been shot, poisoned and infected with diseases such as measles, 'flu or whooping cough which they cannot survive as they have never been in contact with them before.

In 1900 the Nambiquara people numbered over 10 000 in the Amazon forest. There are now about 500. They understand the delicate natural balance of the forest and how to use it without destroying it.

The rain forest helps to ensure an even water supply. Trees allow rainwater to pass through slowly to feed rivers and irrigation systems. The removal of trees allows rainwater to run off quickly, taking soil with it to silt up dams and reservoirs. It causes flooding in the wetter seasons and drought in the drier seasons. Many millions of people are affected.

Eventually, the weather patterns of the whole earth may be affected. The burning of the rain forests adds to the amount of carbon dioxide in the atmosphere and causes it to warm up. This could cause some of the ice to melt at the North and South Poles and make the sea level rise by 10 metres or so. Many big cities would be flooded.

The plants and animals of the rain forest benefit medicine. Drugs for the treatment of leukaemia and cancer, and medicine to help in modern surgery, have been developed from rainforest products. There may be more drugs which could be developed too, but if the forests are destroyed, we shall never know.

The forest is rarely exploited wisely. The loggers only want about 5% of the trees but they damage about 65% of those remaining. The land which has been cleared for logging or ranching or farming or for building roads soon gets eroded by the heavy rain and becomes useless for anything. So they leave this ruined land and go and clear some more forest.

There are plants which grow in the rain forest which might help to develop better varieties elsewhere – new varieties of rice, for example which may be hardier or more resistant to disease. There may be plants similar to the *copaiba* tree which, it has recently been discovered, yields a heavy oil suitable for use in truck engines.

Burning trees in the Amazon forest

❶ State six reasons why every effort should be made to preserve as much of the rain forest as possible.

❷ Suppose enough ice at the North and South Poles melted to raise sea levels by 10 metres (just over 30 feet) throughout the world. Apart from flooding London, what other effects would it have in the UK?

❸ Not everyone has the same view as to whether the Amazon rain forest should be cut down and used for other purposes. Together with a friend decide what each of the following might think and write a paragraph supporting their point of view:
• Miguel Lopez, a farmer in North-east Brazil whose landlord has turned him off his farm.
• Pedro Vadel, a road construction worker on a highway through the forest.
• Peri, one of the Nambiquara people living in the forest.
• Wayne Mackay, a director of a large American mining company.
• Mary Turner, a tourist from Britain.
• Louise Harding, a medical research worker.

The Brazilian government now has a new policy. It says it will only give grants to plans which preserve 50% of the forest in the area being developed.

❹   Work in pairs and discuss whether this is a good policy. Give reasons for your decision.

3 A CHANGE OF SCENE

The use of land in a country changes as the needs of the people change. How might one family be affected by such changes?

The position of Bijlmermeer showing when areas were built

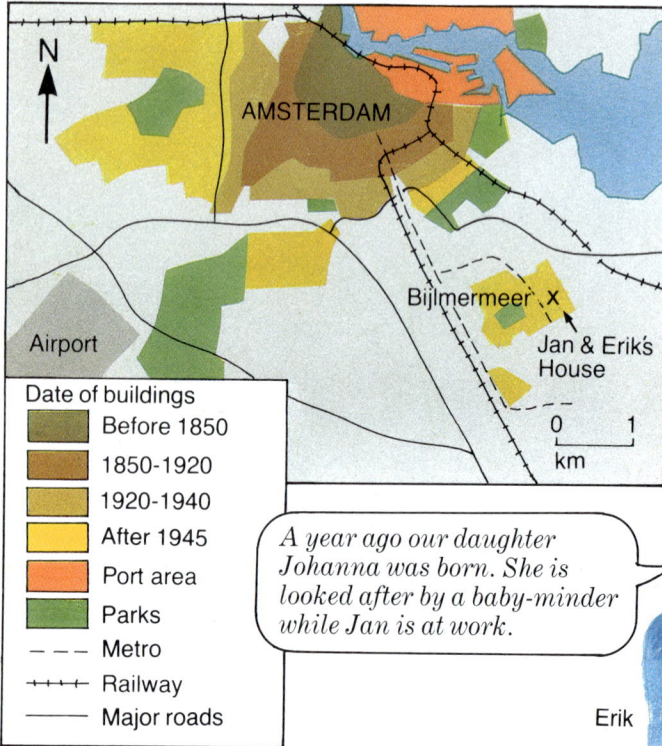

Date of buildings
- Before 1850
- 1850-1920
- 1920-1940
- After 1945
- Port area
- Parks
- – – – Metro
- ++++ Railway
- —— Major roads

We are Jan and Erik Maas. We are both 25 years old and live in Amsterdam in the Netherlands. Soon after we were married four years ago, we came to live in a two bedroom apartment in the Bijlmermeer high-rise estate on the outskirts of Amsterdam.

We feel that as Johanna grows up we would prefer to live in a house with a garden. We are looking for a suitable home within travelling distance of the centre of Amsterdam.

Jan

A year ago our daughter Johanna was born. She is looked after by a baby-minder while Jan is at work.

I work in a Bank and Erik works in a Tourist Information Office, both of which are in the centre of Amsterdam. We travel to work on the metro line which runs through the estate on elevated tracks.

Erik

The Bijlmermeer Estate – notice the elevated railway which runs through the estate.

18

In the city centre are a series of tree-lined canals which are bordered by 16th and 17th century houses. Of the 40 000 historic buildings in the Netherlands, nearly 7 800, or more than 17%, are in Amsterdam. Many are now in need of renovation, the cost of which is enormous. It is very expensive to live in one of these houses, which are among the most attractive in Europe.

Amsterdam is also a city of culture, there is the Rijksmuseum, the Van Gogh Museum and Rembrandt's house as well as a bubbling night life centred around the Leidseplein.

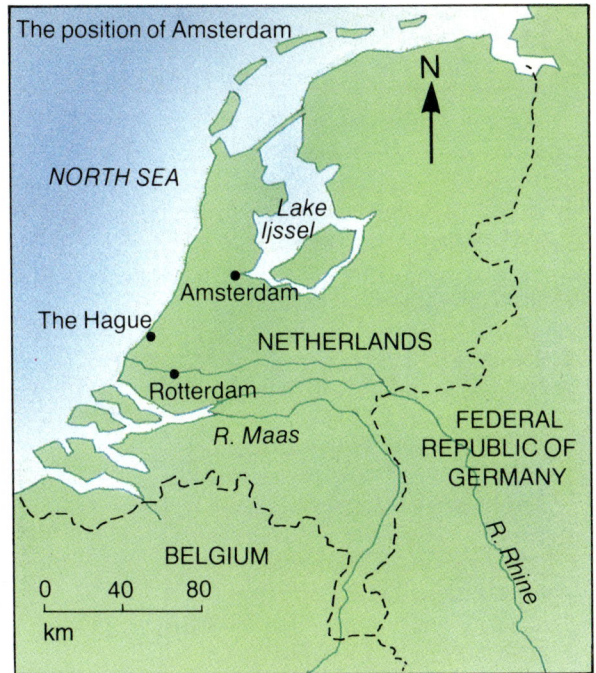

The position of Amsterdam

NORTH SEA

Lake Ijssel

Amsterdam

The Hague

NETHERLANDS

Rotterdam

R. Maas

FEDERAL REPUBLIC OF GERMANY

R. Rhine

BELGIUM

| 0 | 40 | 80 |

km

❶ Using the map of the position of Bijlmermeer on the opposite page:
ⓐ Write down when the estate was built.
ⓑ Measure how far Jan and Erik have to travel to work each day.

❷ Using the photograph of Bijlmermeer to help you, write down:
ⓐ two good features of the estate;
ⓑ two poor features of the estate.

❸ Explain why Jan and Erik want to move.

❹ Using your atlas and the map above:
ⓐ Give three facts which describe the location of Amsterdam.
ⓑ Which direction is Amsterdam from London?
ⓒ How far is Amsterdam from London?

❺ Work with a friend.
ⓐ Use the information on this page to help you design a poster to attract visitors to Amsterdam. Try to tell them as much as you know about the city.
ⓑ List as many reasons as you can why people may decide to move home.

RENOVATED houses along one of the canals in Central Amsterdam

The Randstad

The Randstad is a ring of cities in the western Netherlands. In their centre is the 'Green Heart', a rural area which is increasingly being used for RECREATION and for building. Many people like ourselves are looking for a home with a garden in attractive surroundings. They are moving to the Green Heart, or to nearby areas with pleasant landscape. However, they are still working in the cities and more and more people are travelling by car, causing traffic CONGESTION and parking problems in the cities.

Jan

Randstad area

Built up areas in the Randstad

1956

1986

0   25   50
Km

N

Amsterdam

GREEN HEART

C   B   D

Population in millions

	0	1	2	3	4	5	6	7	8	9	10	11	12	13	14
1956															
1986															

Randstad   Rest of Holland

❶ Look at your atlas and the map of the Randstad and name the cities marked **B**, **C** and **D**.

❷ Read what Jan says above. Then describe what happens in the cities as people move out to the Green Heart by linking the correct halves of the phrases below. The first has been done for you:

Parking problems   in morning and
Green Heart being   evening
Heavy traffic   smaller in size
Cities become   during the day
                          built up

❸ Look at the map of the central area of Amsterdam.
ⓐ Describe the route Erik might take from X, where he enters the city, to Y, where he works, if he travelled by car from the Green Heart.
ⓑ Why it is difficult for Erik to take a direct route?
ⓒ Why is the centre always so congested with traffic when Erik is travelling to and from work?
ⓓ Give one way, shown on the map, in which the Amsterdam planners are trying to help the traffic flow.

CENTRAAL STATION

TRAM- BUS EN METRO STATION

DAM

CENTRUM

Y

NIEUWMARKT

WATERLOO PLEIN

REMBRANDTS PLEIN

X

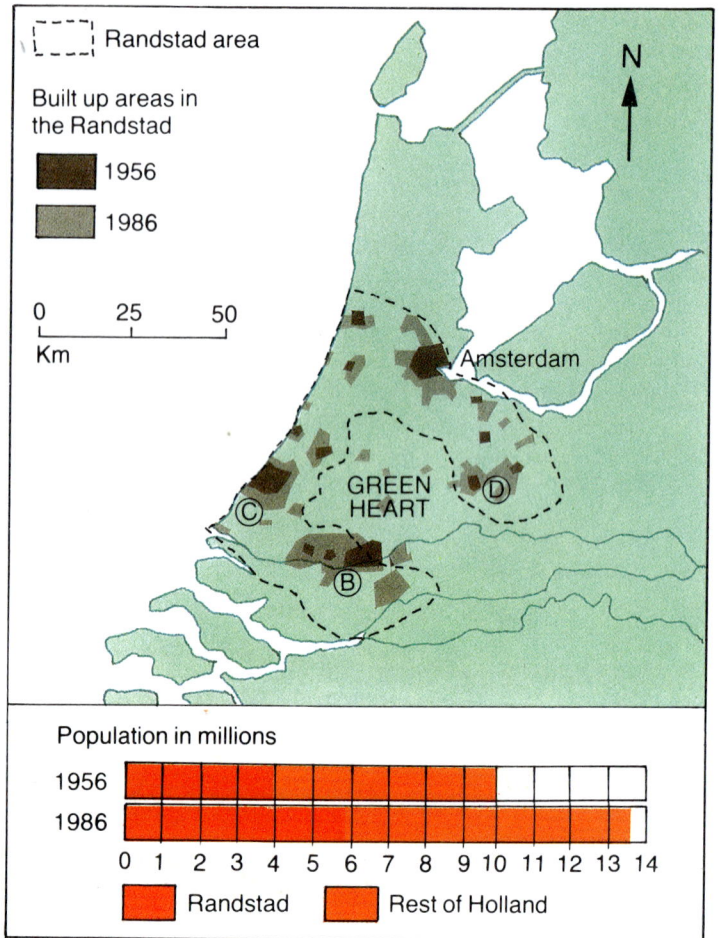

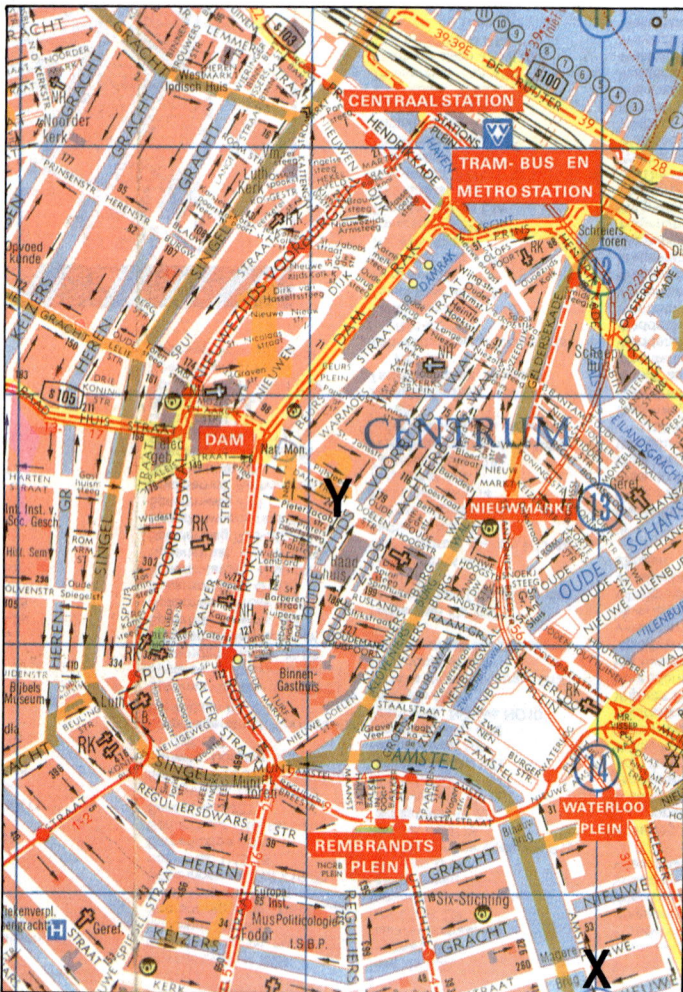

Map of Central Amsterdam

New homes for old in Amsterdam

Jan

As people leave the inner city areas these become more rundown. Amsterdam has a youthful population who are often unable to spend a lot of money on their houses as they are just starting work. Homes are small, streets are narrow and there is little open space. To improve conditions and to attract people back into the city, Amsterdam City Authorities have bought up whole neighbourhoods for development.

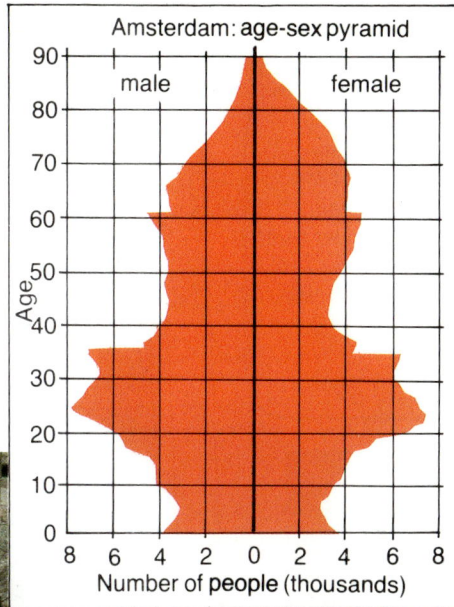

Amsterdam: age-sex pyramid

male   female

Age

Number of **people** (thousands)

❹ Look at the age-sex pyramid for Amsterdam. From the age groups 0–20, 20–40, 40–60, 60–80:
ⓐ Which age group has the largest number of people in Amsterdam?
ⓑ Which two age groups have the smallest number of people in Amsterdam?

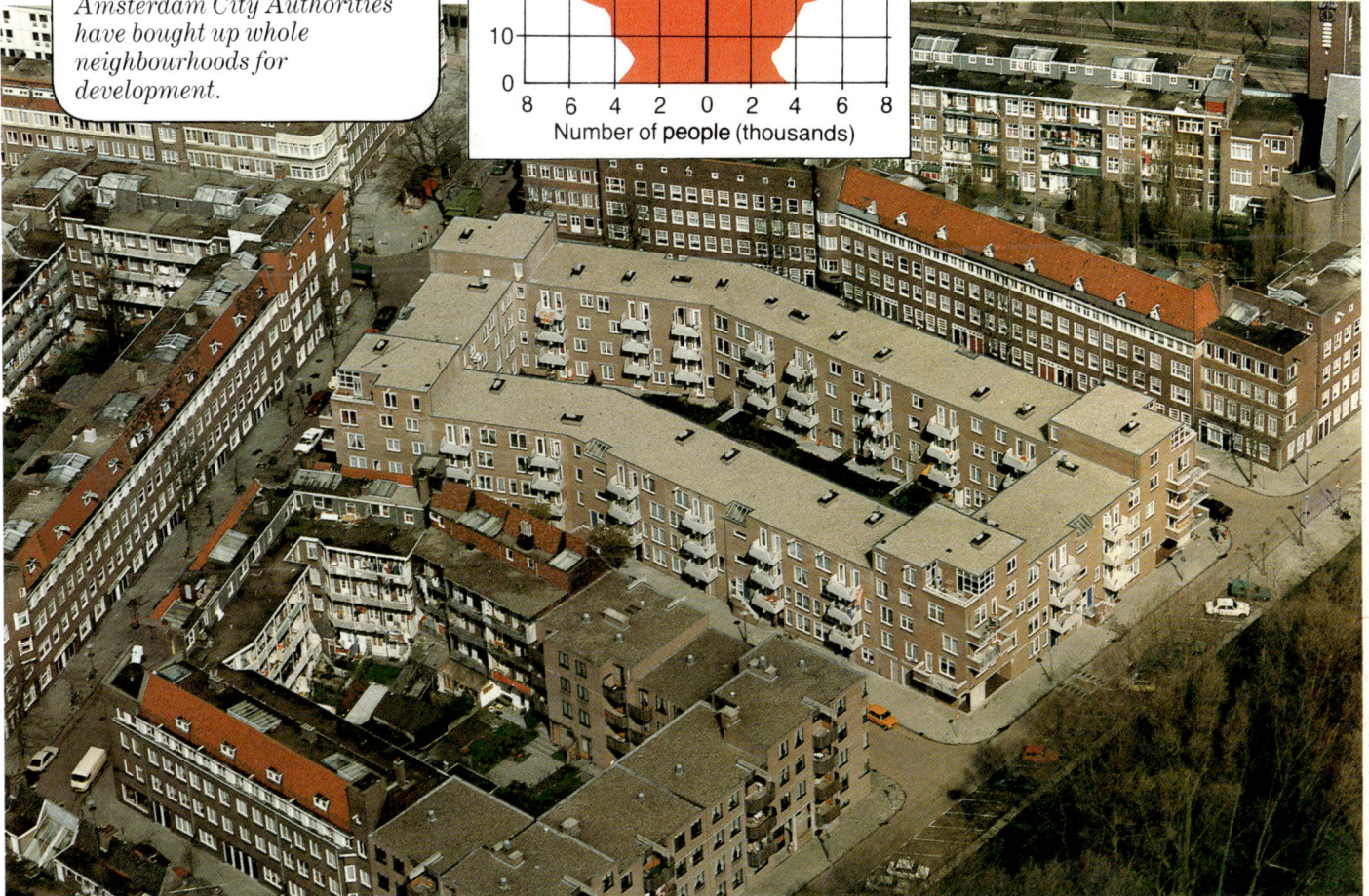

The inner city area of East Amsterdam which was once a mass of old houses has now been replaced by ...

❺ Copy and complete the caption to the photograph above by describing the type of housing which has replaced the old housing. You will need to write *three* sentences and include words like FLATS, STOREYS, COURTYARD, BALCONY etc.

❻ How does Amsterdam hope that such developments will help to solve the problems caused by people leaving the city?

❼ *Imagine that you lived in one of the old houses in East Amsterdam, which is to be renovated by the City Council. The council have told you that they have bought the house which you rent and that you must move. They have agreed to pay you some money to help you move.*
ⓐ *Discuss with your neighbour how you would feel about this.*
ⓑ *Make a list of the advantages and disadvantages of the move to a new flat.*

21

Polderland

Many Dutch people visit my office to ask for information about the new land called the Isselmeer POLDERS. This was made when parts of the sea inlet to the north east of Amsterdam were drained. Polders provide land for agriculture and building, as well as opportunities for recreation.

Erik

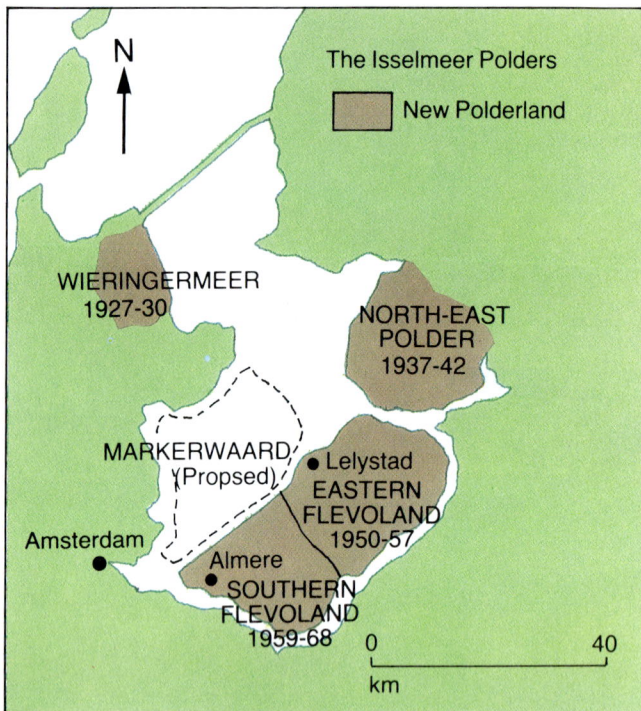

The Isselmeer Polders

□ New Polderland

WIERINGERMEER 1927-30

NORTH-EAST POLDER 1937-42

MARKERWAARD (Propsed)

Lelystad
EASTERN FLEVOLAND 1950-57

Amsterdam

Almere
SOUTHERN FLEVOLAND 1959-68

0 ———— 40 km

In the very heart of the Netherlands lies Flevoland with plenty of room and endless opportunities for recreation.

Anglers, nature-lovers, water sports enthusiasts, campers, roadside picnickers – in fact tourists with all kinds of interests – are catered for in Flevoland. It certainly is a magnificent recreational area and it is easily accessible, being fairly near most of the large towns.

Nearly 100 000 hectares of new land: a paradise for cyclists, with some 500 kilometres of cycle tracks winding through vast stretches of woods, orchards, fields and pastures, past lakes and canals, and sometimes even bulbfields.

❶ The Dutch people's ideas on how the polders should be used have changed. To find out how, use the map of land use in southern Flevoland opposite, to work out the percentages of each of the types of land use shown in the table on the right. Take a copy of the table and complete the column for southern Flevoland. To do this:

ⓐ Count the number of squares which cover southern Flevoland (if more than half, or half a square is in the area, count it, if less than half a square is in the area, do not count it).

ⓑ Count the number of squares covering each land use.

ⓒ Use this formula to find the different percentages of land use:

$$\frac{\text{No. of squares of land use (e.g. all agricultural squares)}}{\text{No. of squares covering southern Flevoland}} \times 100$$

❷ ⓐ Using the map of the Isselmeer Polders:
ⓑ Which is the oldest and which is the newest polder?
ⓒ What changes does your table show for each land use from the oldest to the newest polder?

Land use on the Isselmeer polders (percentages)

Type of land use	Wieringer-meer	North-east Polder	Eastern Flevoland	Southern Flevoland
Agriculture	87	87	75	—
Woods, nature reserves	3	5	11	—
Residential, industrial	1	1	8	—
Dykes, roads, water	9	7	6	7

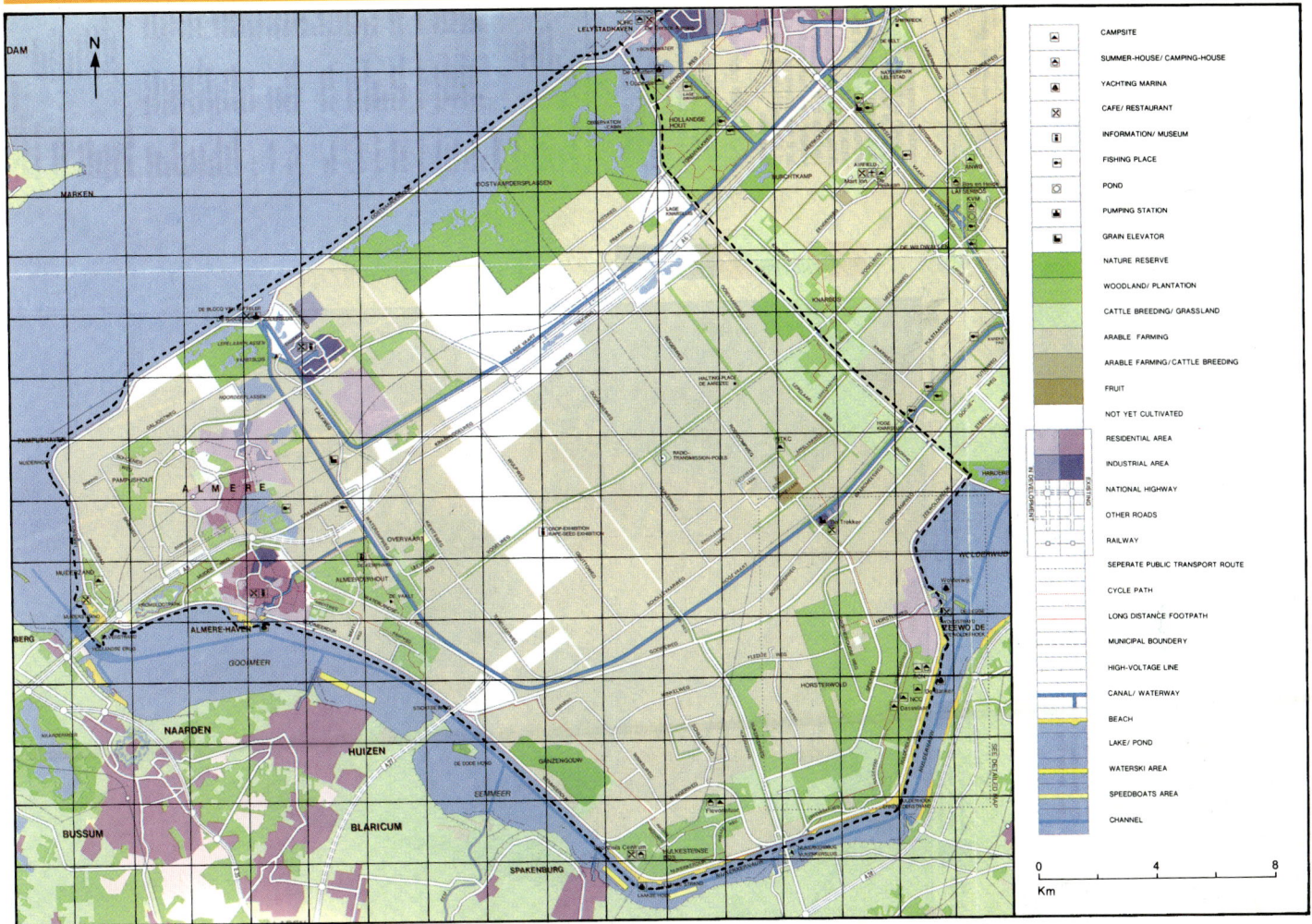

The legend of the map contains the following symbols and categories:

- CAMPSITE
- SUMMER-HOUSE/ CAMPING-HOUSE
- YACHTING MARINA
- CAFE/ RESTAURANT
- INFORMATION/ MUSEUM
- FISHING PLACE
- POND
- PUMPING STATION
- GRAIN ELEVATOR
- NATURE RESERVE
- WOODLAND/ PLANTATION
- CATTLE BREEDING/ GRASSLAND
- ARABLE FARMING
- ARABLE FARMING/CATTLE BREEDING
- FRUIT
- NOT YET CULTIVATED
- RESIDENTIAL AREA
- INDUSTRIAL AREA
- NATIONAL HIGHWAY
- OTHER ROADS
- RAILWAY
- SEPERATE PUBLIC TRANSPORT ROUTE
- CYCLE PATH
- LONG DISTANCE FOOTPATH
- MUNICIPAL BOUNDERY
- HIGH-VOLTAGE LINE
- CANAL/ WATERWAY
- BEACH
- LAKE/ POND
- WATERSKI AREA
- SPEEDBOATS AREA
- CHANNEL

Scale: 0 — 4 — 8 Km

Land use map of southern Flevoland

❸ The Markerwaard, the last polder to be drained, is still under water. The Dutch people are finding it difficult to decide whether or not to go ahead with draining. The arguments for and against are given below.

for

- It would provide high quality agricultural land to make up for land lost elsewhere to building and recreation.

- It could be used for new towns.

- It could provide new possibilities for recreation.

- It could create new nature reserves and forestry.

against

- It would be very expensive to drain.

- The Netherlands do not need new land for agriculture, especially as the European Common Market has too much of the crops that would be produced.

- Many people use this area for water sports with large boats: it is already a valuable recreation area.

- It is used for fishing and some water birds will decrease in number.

❹ Decide whether you are for *or* against draining the Markerwaard polder. List the reasons for your decision. Join with three others to discuss your ideas. Write a group report (covering the arguments for and against) and present it to the rest of the class.

Almere – New Town

Housing in Almere

On a trip to southern Flevoland we visited Almere – a New Town which was begun in 1975. It has a good rail and road link with Amsterdam.

About two-thirds of the people living in Almere came from Amsterdam. Over half of these people still work in Amsterdam even though there are many new industries and offices around Almere. There is a long waiting list for homes in the New Town.

Almere is set out very attractively with lots of parks and green spaces separating different residential areas. Each area has its own shopping centre. Most of the homes are single family houses and there are a few flats. The town already has cafés and restaurants, a sports centre, a swimming bath, a library and a good bus service.

Jan

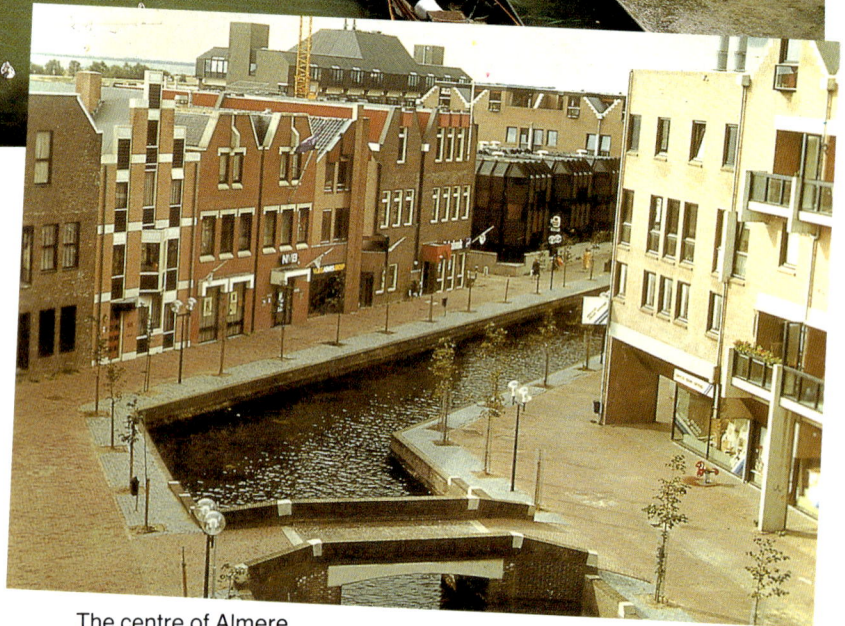

The centre of Almere

❶ Write down five words which best describe the centre of Almere shown in the photograph above.

❷ Write two sentences to describe the houses shown in the top photograph.

Erik

Now that Johanna is getting older we are thinking of having a second child. We will need more room and I'd like a place with a garden. If we moved to Almere we would have to wait for our house to be built and we would then both have a longer and more expensive journey to work. Both Jan and I have always lived in the city so we are unsure about what to do. Some of our friends have moved to Almere.

Other houses are available in other parts of Amsterdam and also on the Bijlmermeer Estate where we live at the moment.

KEY

++++ Railway

— Main roads

Water

Residential areas 1–5

Industrial areas

3   4   2   ALMERE   1   5

0   5
km

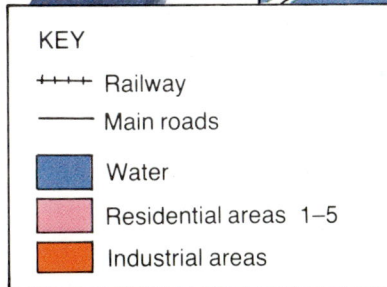

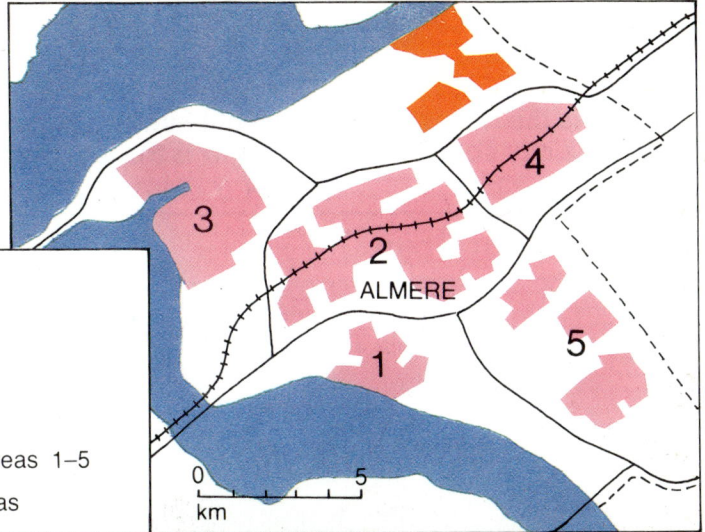

Almere under construction, looking south, in the background, Lake Gool and the town of Huizen on the 'old land'.

❸ Write three sentences about the layout of Almere using the photograph and map above.

❹ In pairs:
ⓐ Make a list of all the things you would look for in a home if you were Jan and Erik.
ⓑ Decide which of the following possible homes you think Jan and Erik should choose.
   (i) A home in the inner city area of Amsterdam?
   (ii) A larger apartment in the Bijlmermeer Estate?
   (iii) A home in Almere?
Give reasons for your choice and discuss them with others.

Why not investigate?

Look around the town or city in or near where you live. Choose a small area where housing has either been renovated or where there is new housing. Prepare a folder of work on this area. Here are some suggestions:

● Mark the area you have chosen on a map of the town.
● Find out what the area was like 50 years ago. (You could ask older residents or visit your local library.)
● Prepare a questionnaire to find out about the people who live there now – Do they own their own homes? What age group are they in? Where did they live before they moved to the area? Where do they shop, play sport, or go for entertainment?

Present your results in the form of maps, age-sex pyramids and graphs.

4 A NEW BOMBAY

Bombay is the richest city in India but has the largest slums in Asia. Why is the city so overcrowded? How is the city planning for its future?

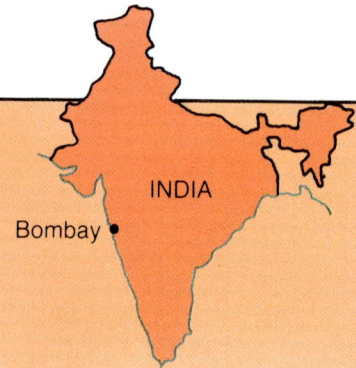

INDIA

Bombay

The Taj Mahal Inter-Continental India's most famous hotel ... quite simply, like few others in the world. 650 air-conditioned rooms and suites. 3 speciality restaurants, 2 bars, a coffee shop. Swimming pool. Splendid conference and banquet rooms and facilities.

❶ ⓐ Which of these illustrations of Bombay surprises you most? Discuss your answer with a friend.
ⓑ Pick out details from this page which show:
(i) wealth, (ii) poverty and (iii) overcrowding in Bombay.

NO ROOM FOR THE HOMELESS

Anne Smith, who has visited India, begins a series today in which she investigates the enormous increase in the population of Bombay.

I watched in horror today as bulldozers flattened a slum settlement (which are known as 'zopadpattis' in Bombay). It was not difficult to do. They were flimsy dwellings made of bamboo, metal sheets, plastic bags and any waste material which might be available.

The people, most of whom had come into Bombay from the countryside in recent years, watched in helpless anger. They had built these homes for themselves. No warning had been given. No time was allowed to rescue food and possessions.

One man told me he was a carpenter. He had lost his tools and would never find work without them.

'Too many people'

I asked an official why they took such drastic measures. 'Too many people are coming to live in Bombay' he said, 'We must stop it. Those who came before 1976 are protected'.

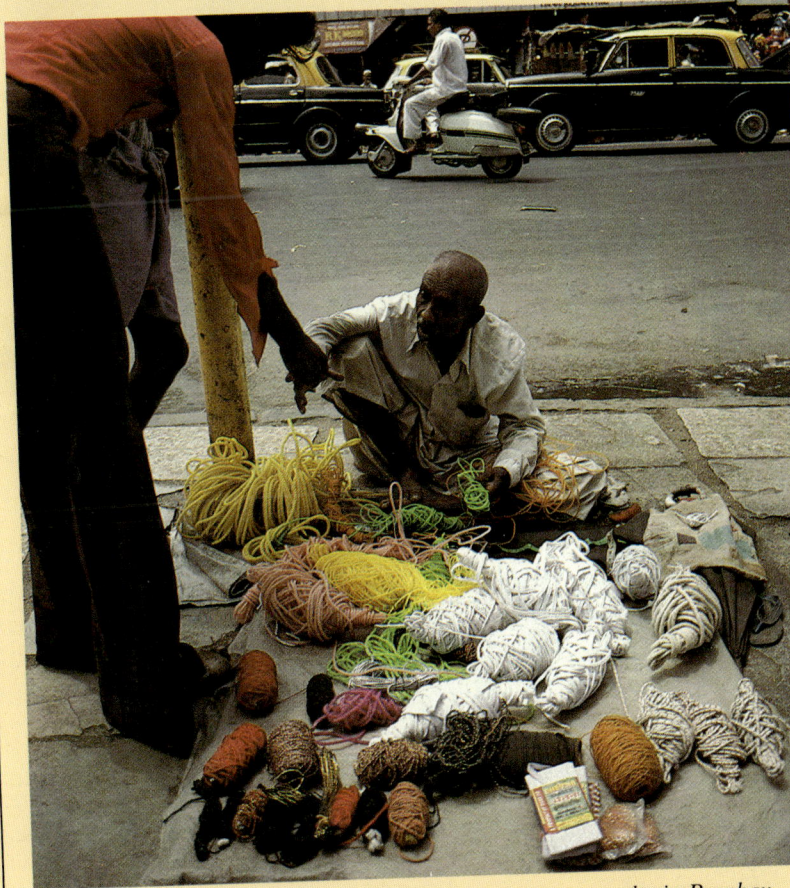

Anne Smith

There are 4.5 million people in Bombay's slums. About 2 million of them have arrived since 1976 and have no rights at all.

The people have tried to use the law to prevent the demolition. In 1985, however, the Supreme Court of India ruled that it was legal to clear away slum settlements.

'More than we can afford'

I asked people at the site whether the council provided any housing. 'They build blocks of flats', I was told, 'but there are too few of them and they cost far more than we can afford'. I wondered what they would do now. 'We will build our houses again on the same spot'.

Very few people have no work. A man living in the poorest house may be helping to build a large office block during the day. Thirty-five per cent of the slum dwellers are self-employed. They sell vegetables or flowers or cigarettes. They reclaim waste rags or plastic. Thirty-eight per cent earn wages in factories or on building sites or as domestic servants. Twenty per cent of all the council workers live in slums.

Bombay is a wealthy city. It has 1% of India's population but pays 30% of its income tax. But the official said 'The rule of law must be upheld'.

A street trader in Bombay

❷ Read the newspaper article, then write a sentence to answer each of the following questions:
ⓐ What do the slum dwellers use to build their homes?
ⓑ Why does the council want to destroy their homes?
ⓒ Why do the slum dwellers have to build their own homes?
ⓓ In what ways would Bombay suffer if the slum dwellers left?

❸ If you were a rich person in Bombay, in what ways would you be:
ⓐ glad to see slum dwellers go;
ⓑ sorry to lose them?
Give reasons for your answers.

Life in the countryside

More food is being grown in India than ever before. But life in the countryside is still difficult.
Many people are leaving the countryside for cities like Bombay.

FEEDING OUR PEOPLE – NO MORE FAMINE

India's farmers are growing more food then ever before. They are growing more rice, more wheat, more cereals of every kind.

This has been achieved by the High Yielding Varieties Programme which we introduced. Scientists have produced seeds which will yield more food from every farm if they are looked after properly.

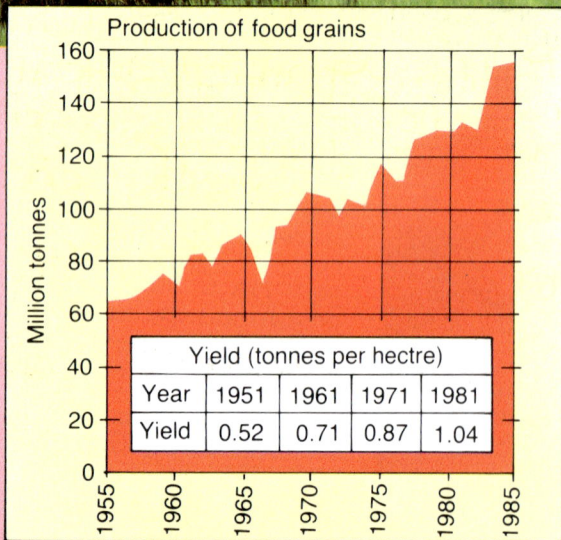

Production of food grains

Yield (tonnes per hectre)				
Year	1951	1961	1971	1981
Yield	0.52	0.71	0.87	1.04

The new seeds need:
- a carefully controlled water supply
- plenty of fertiliser
- sprays against insects and diseases.

To help farmers the government has provided:
- supplies of new seeds to sell to farmers
- advice and training for farmers
- loans.

A measure of the success of the government's plan has been that in 1966, India imported 10 million tonnes of grain. In 1984 there was a surplus of 8 million tonnes. Some of this was exported.

❶ ⓐ Look at the table showing grain yield. How did it change between 1951 and 1981?
ⓑ How did the change come about?

❷ Design a poster which might be displayed in an Indian village to persuade farmers to use high-yielding varieties of seeds.

❸ What was the production of food grains in
(i) 1955
(ii) 1970
(iii) 1985?

❹ Why do you think India needed to import grain in 1966?

IT'S A HARD LIFE, O BROTHERS

Anne Smith continues her reports by visiting the countryside near Bombay. She finds out why people are leaving the villages.

Anne Smith

I heard this song sung on the streets of Bombay by travelling entertainers. The audience nodded their heads in agreement.

I came to the villages to see how much truth there was in the song. Surely, life was now much better in the countryside.

'WE END UP IN DEBT'
One farmer, Mr Menon, told me that some farmers had gained. 'The new seeds do give a much better crop and there is more for us to sell. But they are expensive. So is the fertiliser and the weedkiller that we have to buy. Many farmers borrow money to buy them. They may end up in debt. The big landowners gain the most'. He added that he had sold his land and was moving to Bombay.

'NO FUTURE ON THE LAND'
I asked if he could work for a big landowner. He said he could, but the work was not regular and was badly paid. More and more machinery was being used.

Another farmer, Mr Bharti, said that he was leaving because his farm was too small. His father had died and the land was divided between his sons. None of them had enough to support their families. 'It is difficult in a good year', he said, 'It is impossible if we have drought or floods which are always likely. There is no future on the land'.

The rise in Bombay's population has much to do with poverty on the land.

> Listen to the workers' tale
> O brothers, O sisters
> With our labour we ploughed the land,
> We sowed the seed,
> We made the earth our bride.
> Our sweat flowed so the landlord could grow fat,
> The landlord's greed drove us out,
> Away from the village to the city,
> Where we now search for every scrap of food.
> And why is that?
> Because it's the feudal rule.
> There's nothing to eat and nothing to drink
> No clothes to wear and nowhere to live. It's a false rule, O brothers,
> A false rule.

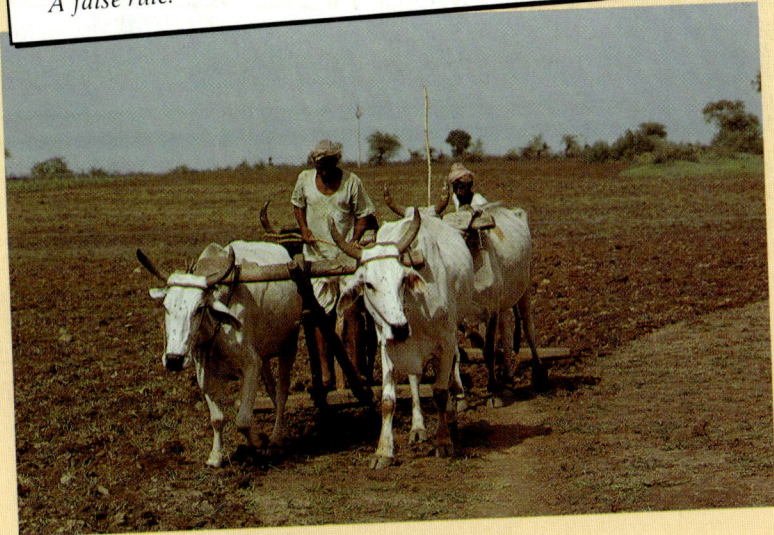

A farming scene near Bombay

THE POPULATION OF BOMBAY IN MILLIONS

YEAR	1911	1921	1931	1941	1951	1961	1971	1981	*1986
POPULATION	1.1	1.4	1.4	1.8	3.0	4.2	6.0	8.2	8.3

* estimate

5 ⓐ Why do the new seeds not help some farmers?
ⓑ Why do you think the rich landowners gain most?
ⓒ What reasons are given for leaving the land?

6 ⓐ Draw a line graph to show the changes in the population of Bombay from 1911 to 1986.
ⓑ Describe carefully what the graph shows.

7 *Suggest ways in which the government might encourage farmers to stay on the land.*

'ANYONE CAN FIND SOME SORT OF WORK HERE'

Anne Smith reports on employment in Bombay.

In 1986, there were about 7500 working factories in Bombay. They included textiles and clothing, engineering, food processing, oil refining, plastics and chemicals. Bombay is also the food capital of India.

I asked Mr Kamar, a Bombay business man, why there is so much industry in the city. 'There are many reasons', he said, 'In the first place, Bombay has always been the Indian port which is nearest to Europe. It has many sources of power. It can easily use oil from the countries bordering the Persian Gulf. Also oil and gas are pumped from wells in the Bombay High oilfield just off the coast. The oil is refined at two refineries in Bombay. They produce petrol, paraffin, diesel oil and other products which we use in making synthetic rubber, plastics, fertilisers and paints.

Power and Industry

We also have plenty of electricity: India's first nuclear power station was built near here. Hydro-electricity is generated in the mountains behind the city. The heavy rainfall and steep slopes are ideal for it.

Bombay has 1.5 million people working for private firms whether in factories or offices or shops. Another 2 million work in the public sector either for the government or the state or local council.

These are workers in the 'formal' sector who work regular hours for a wage. Countless more find work in the 'informal sector'. They are self-employed and earn money by fetching and carrying, buying and selling, mending and making.'

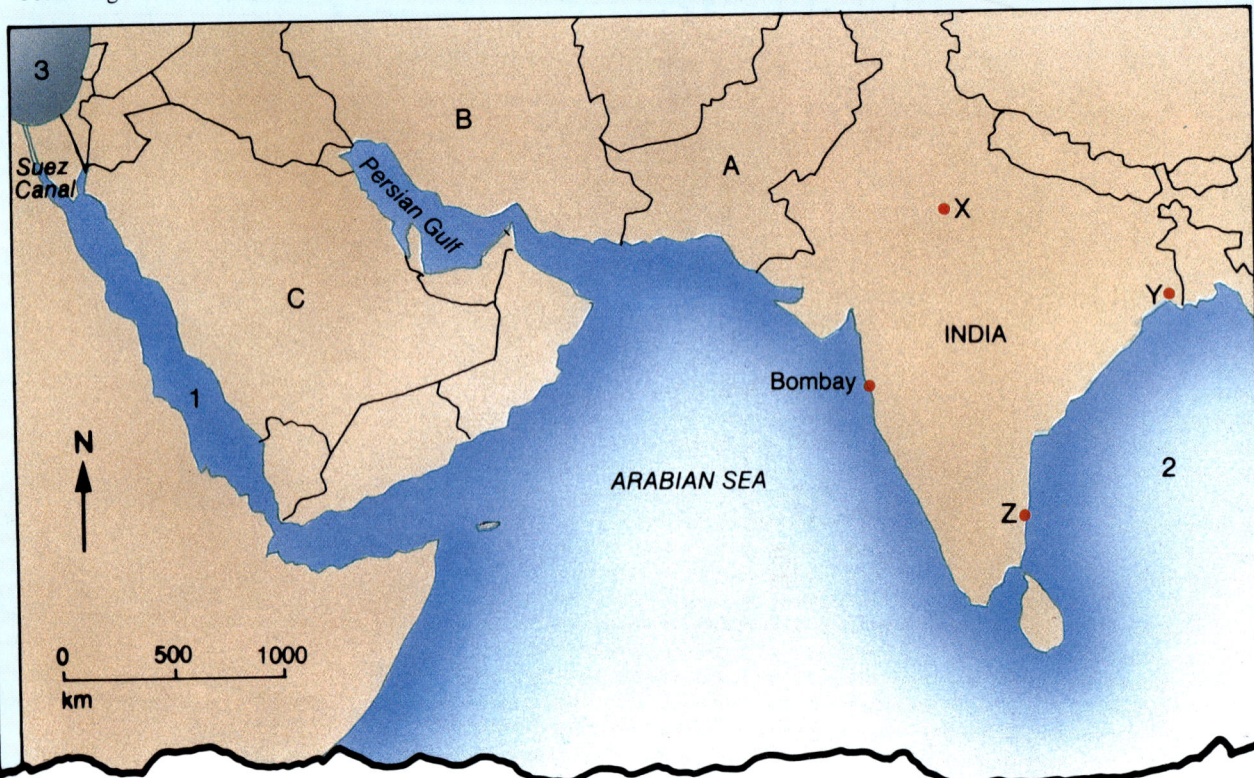

❶ The map above is not fully labelled. Use your atlas to name:
ⓐ the sea areas 1, 2 and 3;
ⓑ the countries A, B and C;
ⓒ the Indian cities X, Y and Z.

❷ Copy and complete:
Bombay is on the _____ coast of India. It is India's second largest city after Calcutta which is _____ kilometres away in a _____ _____ direction. Bombay is on the coast of the _____ Sea.

Formal work – a film studio in Bombay

Informal work – a simple pottery in a poor housing area of Bombay

Employment in formal work in Bombay (%)

Industry	41
Trade and commerce	22
Services	20
Transport	11
Other (e.g. building)	6
TOTAL	100

Employment in industry in Bombay

Type of industry	Number of factories	Workers (thousands)
Textiles	603	235
Transport equipment	166	55
Metals	710	40
Chemicals	368	38
Machinery	461	33
Electrical machinery	296	30
Printing	436	20

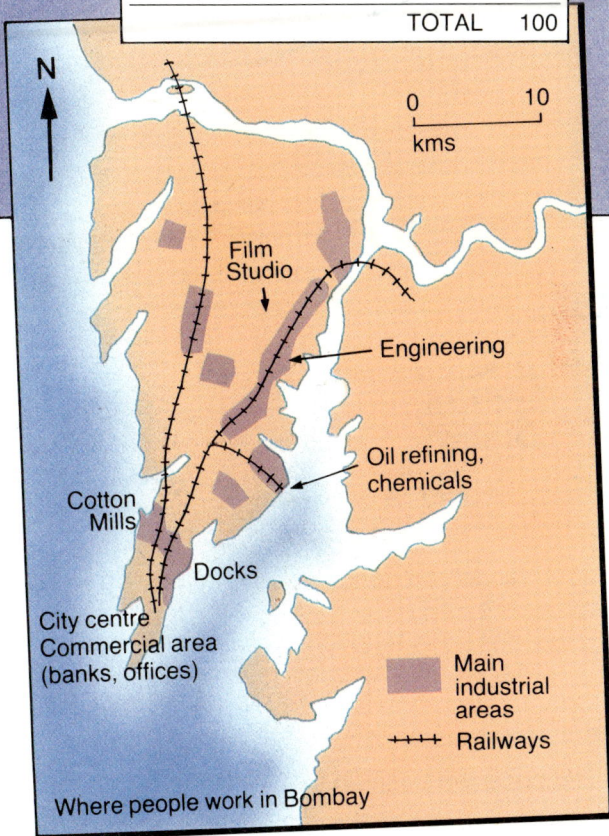

Where people work in Bombay

N

0   10
kms

Film Studio

Engineering

Oil refining, chemicals

Cotton Mills

Docks

City centre
Commercial area
(banks, offices)

Main industrial areas
+++ Railways

❸ Read the newspaper article opposite.
ⓐ Name three sources of power that may be used in Bombay.
ⓑ Why do you think oil is important for the growth of industry?

❹ What is the difference between 'formal' and 'informal' work?

❺ Look at the table 'Employment in formal work in Bombay'.

ⓐ Using a circle like the one shown here, draw a pie chart to show employment in formal work in Bombay.

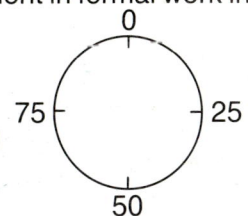

0
75 ─ 25
50

ⓑ The article tells us that 3.5 million people work in the public and private sectors. How many of them are employed in services?

❻ ⓐ Look at the table 'Employment in industry in Bombay' above. The industries are listed in order of the number of workers they employ. Rewrite the type of industry in order of numbers of factories.
ⓑ How can you tell that textile factories are likely to be bigger than those making metals?

❼ How does the map suggest that transport is important to industry in Bombay?

❽ *Suggest what type of work might be found in the city centre.*

Bombay has a plan – for a New Bombay

Come to New Bombay –

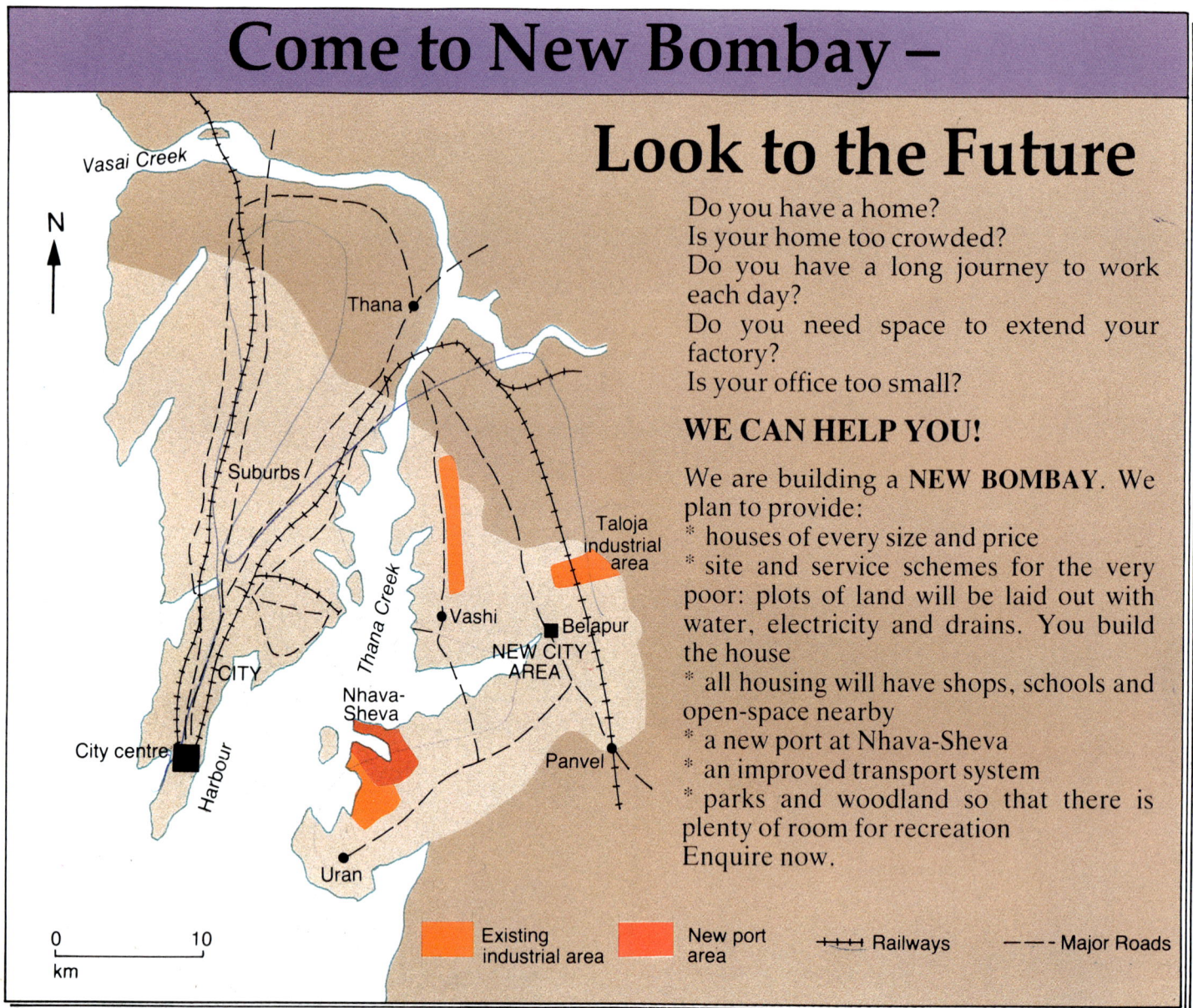

Look to the Future

Do you have a home?
Is your home too crowded?
Do you have a long journey to work each day?
Do you need space to extend your factory?
Is your office too small?

WE CAN HELP YOU!

We are building a **NEW BOMBAY**. We plan to provide:
* houses of every size and price
* site and service schemes for the very poor: plots of land will be laid out with water, electricity and drains. You build the house
* all housing will have shops, schools and open-space nearby
* a new port at Nhava-Sheva
* an improved transport system
* parks and woodland so that there is plenty of room for recreation
Enquire now.

Map labels: Vasai Creek, N, Thana, Suburbs, Taloja industrial area, Vashi, Belapur, NEW CITY AREA, CITY, Nhava-Sheva, City centre, Harbour, Panvel, Thana Creek, Uran

0 — 10 km

Existing industrial area | New port area | ┼┼┼ Railways | – – – Major Roads

1 ⓐ Draw a simple sketch map from the map above to show Bombay city, Bombay suburbs and New Bombay.
  (i) Shade and label each of the three areas.
  (ii) Show the railways and the harbour.
  (iii) Draw and label arrows showing south-west winds blowing towards Bombay.
 ⓑ (i) What do you notice about the position of the harbour? (Clue: direction of wind.)
  (ii) Why do you think the city centre is close to the harbour?
  (iii) Why is it a strange place to have a city centre?
  (iv) How does the position of the city centre help to make roads congested and trains crowded?

2 ⓐ What do you notice about the area on which Bombay is built?
 ⓑ How does this help to make it a crowded city?
 ⓒ How far would a worker have to travel to work from a northern suburb of Bombay to the city centre? Estimate the distance.

3 Describe the position of New Bombay.

4 Which features of the plan for New Bombay are likely to attract:
 ⓐ people to live there,
 ⓑ businessmen to set up businesses?

5 Why is it unlikely that the advertisement would be helpful to slum dwellers?

WILL THE PLAN WORK?

Anne Smith completes her investigation of Bombay by looking at the plan for a New Bombay.

Anne Smith

Indian planners are sure that they have the answer to the difficulties which Bombay has to face. It is New Bombay – a completely new city of 2 million people to be built on the eastern side of Thana Creek on what is mainly farmland.

BIG PROBLEMS

Certainly there is the need for a big answer to some big problems. There are too many people in Bombay now and the situation gets worse every day. There are not enough houses, never mind houses of good quality. The electricity and gas supplies, the drains and the sewers are quite unable to cope.

Every train and bus has passengers hanging on by their finger tips. Every street near the city centre has a permanent traffic jam.

The air has a foul smell. There is very little open space in which to escape for even a short time.

Old cramped factories have no room to modernise or expand.

A start has been made in New Bombay, 125 000 people live in the area. One new township, Vashi has 10 000 families of workers in nearby industries.

There is plenty of space for factories. Rent and rates will be a lot cheaper. But many factories and offices do business with other factories and offices. They may prefer to stay where they are.

Some of the big industries, like oil refining might welcome the chance to build near the new port of Nhava-Sheva.

The houses are a great improvement, but even the site and service schemes are far too expensive for slum dwellers. Those who make a living by selling goods may prefer to stay near the docks or the markets and near their customers in the crowded parts of Bombay.

There are still many doubts. Will the World Bank provide enough money to pay for it all? Will the villagers in New Bombay be willing to give up their land?

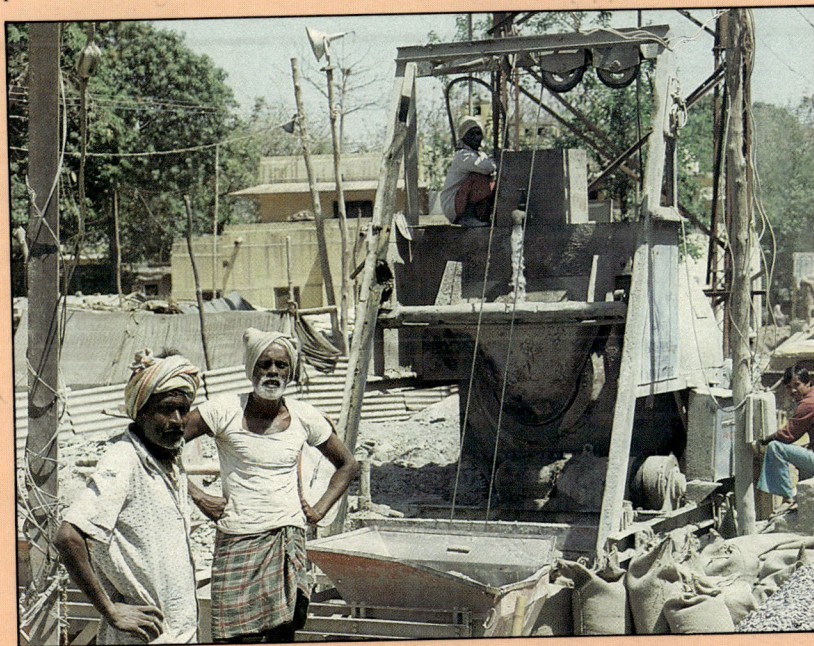

Building work

6 ⓐ Work in groups. Produce a report which tries to show that the New Bombay plan is necessary.
ⓑ Draw up a list of reasons why the following people might be better off moving to New Bombay
    (i) a factory owner
    (ii) a slum dweller
    (iii) a vegetable seller
    (iv) a manager of an oil refinery.
For each one, say why they might not wish to move to New Bombay.

Why not investigate?

Study the building of a New Town in the UK. Describe the ways in which it is (a) similar to and (b) different from New Bombay.

5 INDUSTRIAL GROWTH AND CHANGE

There are many reasons why industries are located in particular places. Why does the growth of one industry tend to attract other industries to the same area? What effect does this concentration have on a region?

Charging the furnace

An opencast iron ore mine

Coal being taken to the steelworks

Iron and Steel making

Three RAW MATERIALS are needed to make iron: IRON ORE, coal and limestone. Iron ore is found as a mineral rock and is QUARRIED from the ground. Coal is needed to heat the iron ore so that it melts and then separates from the rock in which it is found. Limestone helps the separation process which is carried out in a blast furnace. The molten iron or pig iron is drawn off from the bottom of the furnace. When this process first began, much more coal than iron ore was needed.

The iron is made into steel by heating it to very high temperatures. Often other minerals are added to make very high grade steels. The blocks of steel, known as ingots, can then be shaped or rolled out flat in a rolling mill to make steel sheet.

Stages in making steel

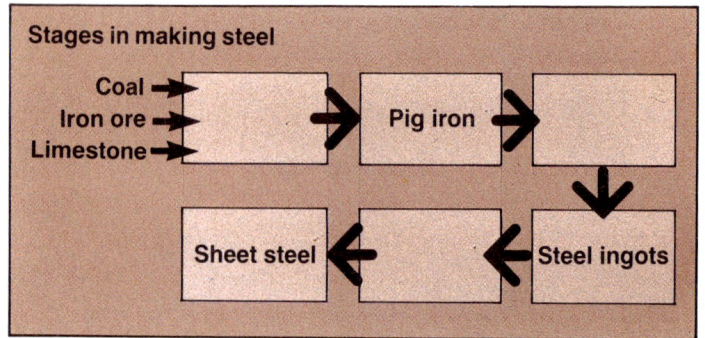

Coal →
Iron ore →
Limestone →
→ Pig iron →
Steel ingots
Sheet steel ←

Locating a steelworks

Location	Coal	Iron ore	Transport	Market	TOTAL
A					
B					
C					
D					

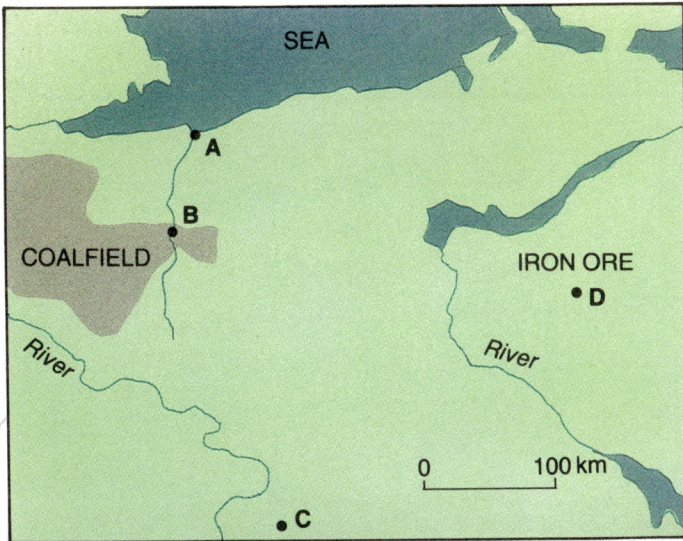

A – a large port on the sea coast
B – a small town on the edge of large coalfield
C – the largest city in the region
D – a small village in an area where iron ore is found

Engineering firms which make tools, machinery and vehicles from metal often build factories near to steelworks. This is particularly true when the metals needed in machine and tool making are also produced in the area. These raw materials are more expensive to transport than the FINISHED PRODUCTS which tend to be small. However, transport to markets (which may be a long way away) is an important consideration.

An engineering firm making cars

❶ Read the information on iron and steel making on the opposite page. Draw the diagram 'Stages in making steel' and use the information to complete it by labelling the three blank boxes.

❷ Study the map above carefully.
ⓐ Imagine that you lived over 100 years ago and have been asked to start an iron and steel industry in the area shown. There are four possible SITES for the works at settlements **A**, **B**, **C** and **D**.
ⓑ To help you to decide, you are asked to draw and complete the table 'Locating a steelworks'. At the top of the columns are four of the main points to consider:
■ Is the site the best for getting coal for the BLAST FURNACE ?
■ Is the site the best for getting iron ore for the blast furnace?
■ Is the site the best for transporting coal and iron ore to the blast furnace, as well as for moving the finished steel to other parts of the country? Remember more coal than iron ore is needed and so it is more costly to transport. Water is the cheapest form of transport but it is also the slowest.

■ Is the site near a good place to sell the steel or in a good position to send it to the MARKET ?
ⓒ Give a mark out of 5 for each of the main points for each site. Add them up in the total column. The best site will be the one with the highest total.
ⓓ Which is the best site for the steelworks?

❸ As the region develops, engineering firms wish to build factories in the area shown on the map. The main considerations for choosing a site for an engineering works are raw materials, transport and markets.
ⓐ Draw a table like the one you used for locating a steelworks but use the headings: *Raw materials, Transport* and *Markets*.
ⓑ Complete the table for locating an engineering factory in the area on the map. It is important to remember where you located your steel works.
ⓒ Suggest which is the best site for an engineering works.

❹ *Imagine that the coal or iron ore located in the area shown on the map ran out. Why might a government try to keep the steel and engineering industries in the region?*

N

0   1000 km

UNION OF SOVIET SOCIALIST REPUBLICS

E

• Moscow

Donetsk •

F

G

H

The position of Donetsk

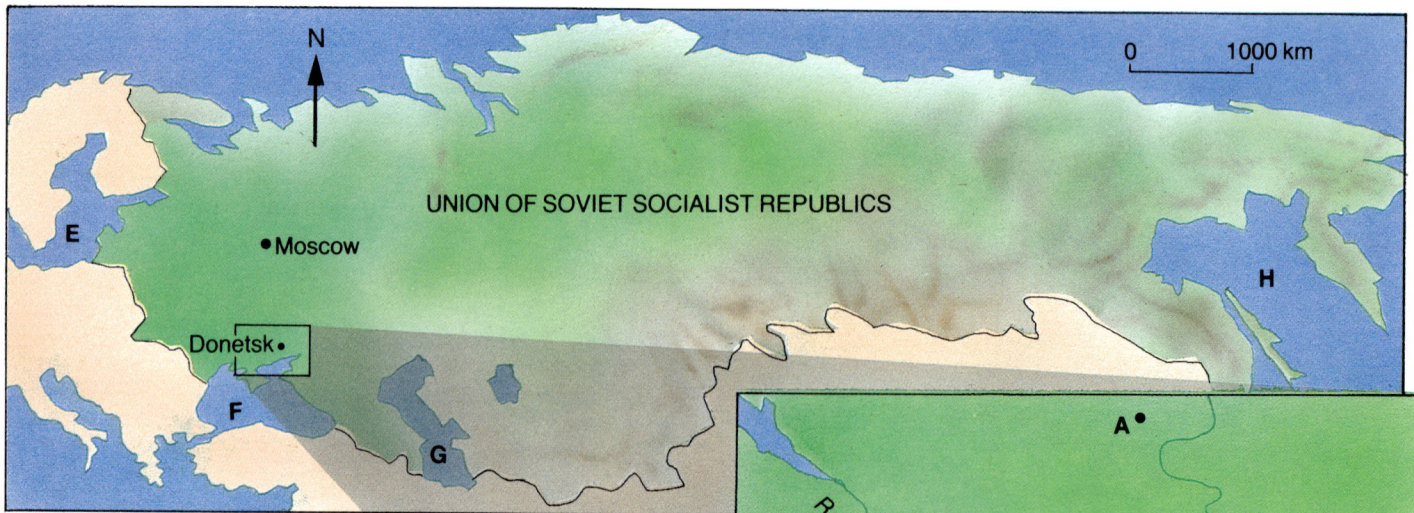

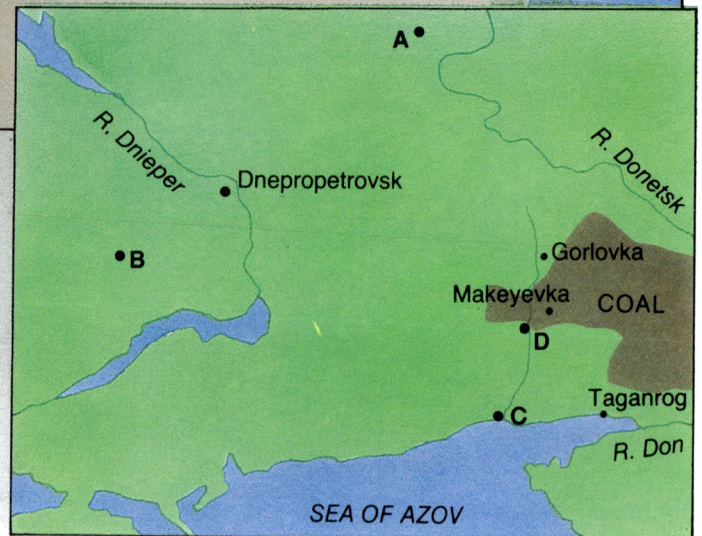

A •

R. Dnieper

• Dnepropetrovsk

R. Donetsk

• B

• Gorlovka

Makeyevka   COAL

• D

Taganrog

• C

R. Don

SEA OF AZOV

John Hughes

A Russian coal and steel city with a Welsh connection

Until 1924 the city of Donetsk, which lies south of Moscow in the USSR, was known as Yuzovka.

Try to say Yuzovka slowly. Say an 'H' instead of the 'Y' — 'Huzovka'. 'Hughes-ovka', but who was Hughes?

John Hughes was born in 1814 in South Wales and worked in the steel and engineering industry. He made his name as director of the Millwall Engineering and Shipbuilding Company.

John Hughes, having visited Russia in the 1860s, reached an agreement with the Russian government to build a rail-rolling factory in the Donetsk area. He was also asked to develop coal mining, iron and rail production and to build a railway to link up with the Kharkov-Azov line.

The equipment shipped from Britain was brought through the Black Sea to Taganrog, the nearest port. Teams of oxen were used for the final stage of the journey.

Hughes chose a location at the western end of the large Donbass coalfield. This was the nearest point on the coalfield to the iron ore deposits at Krivoy Rog. More coal than ore was needed in the blast furnace and it was cheaper to move the ore than the coal. Manganese found nearby could also be used in the process.

The first blast furnace was opened in 1872 and by 1876, Yuzovski Zavoa (the factory) was the largest works of its kind in Russia.

John Hughes died in St Petersburg in 1889 but his four sons continued to manage the works. There were many strikes and finally with the Revolution in 1917 the Welsh connection ended.

Later the town, now a city, was renamed Donetsk, but one area of the town is still known as Yuzovka. Even today, in Leninskaya street, there are some typical British houses of red brick called the three- or four-rouble houses, because that was the rent charged for them.

The History of Donetsk from 1918

1918 – 1921
Civil War in which Russian people from different political groups fought one another. The Union of Soviet Socialist Republics was founded and Russia became a communist country.

1922 – 1940
Soviet planning stressed the need for heavy industry such as coal, steel and engineering. Stalin introduced Five-Year Industrial Plans from 1928 onwards. Yuzovka grew quickly with much new railway construction.

1924
Yuzovka changes its name to Stalino.

1941 – 1945
Second World War. Stalino was occupied by German troops and greatly damaged.

1945 – 1960
As part of government planning Stalino was rebuilt and its industries revived: steel-making, coal production, machine building, mining and constructional equipment repair and building material manufacture, chemical plants and the metallurgical industry all thrived.

1961
Stalino changes it name to Donetsk.

1987
Donetsk today continues to develop new industries and related businesses. These include a textile works, a toy factory, food processing and industrial and scientific planning institutions.

A textile factory in Donetsk

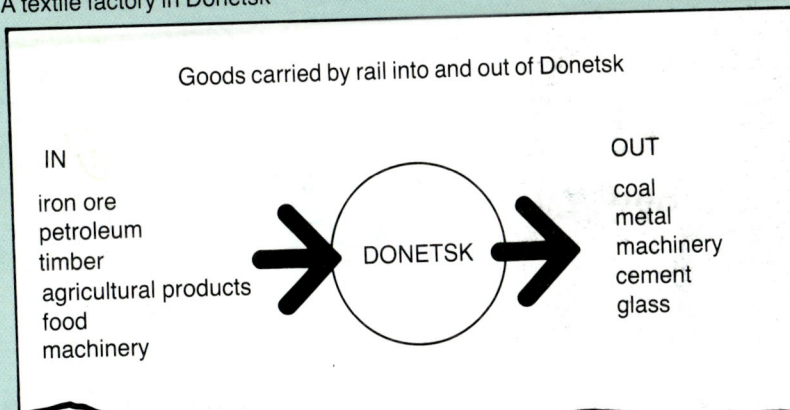

Goods carried by rail into and out of Donetsk

IN

iron ore
petroleum
timber
agricultural products
food
machinery

DONETSK

OUT

coal
metal
machinery
cement
glass

❶ ⓐ Compare the map 'The position of Donetsk' with the map you used for locating a steelworks on page 35. What do you notice about them?
ⓑ How closely does the location of Donetsk resemble your choice of location?
ⓒ What are the real names of places **A**, **B**, **C** and **D**?
ⓓ The Sea of Azov is part of which sea?

❷ Look at the map of the USSR and using your atlas:
ⓐ Name the seas marked E, F, G and H.
ⓑ Name five countries which border the USSR.
ⓒ Calculate how far it is across the USSR from east to west.
ⓓ Calculate how far Donetsk is from Moscow.

❸ Read the article on page 36 carefully.
ⓐ Give two reasons why John Hughes choose Donetsk as the site for the steelworks.

ⓑ Use your atlas to describe the route of the ships bringing the equipment from the UK to Taganrog.

❹ Look at the history of Donetsk above.
ⓐ What type of industry was developed from 1922 to 1940?
ⓑ What type of industry developed from 1945 to 1960?
ⓒ What types of industry developed after 1960?

❺ How do the goods carried into Donetsk by rail differ from those taken out of Donetsk?

❻ List three reasons why a large engineering industry developed in Donetsk.

❼ *Use the history of Donetsk above to describe the part the government has played in the development of Donetsk.*

A region of industry

As industries grow they need good transport to bring raw materials to the works and to take FINISHED PRODUCTS to market. Heavy industry like coal, steel and heavy engineering often uses rail transport. Towns with heavy industry develop good rail transport and this attracts more industry to the area. Often the largest towns have the most rail links.

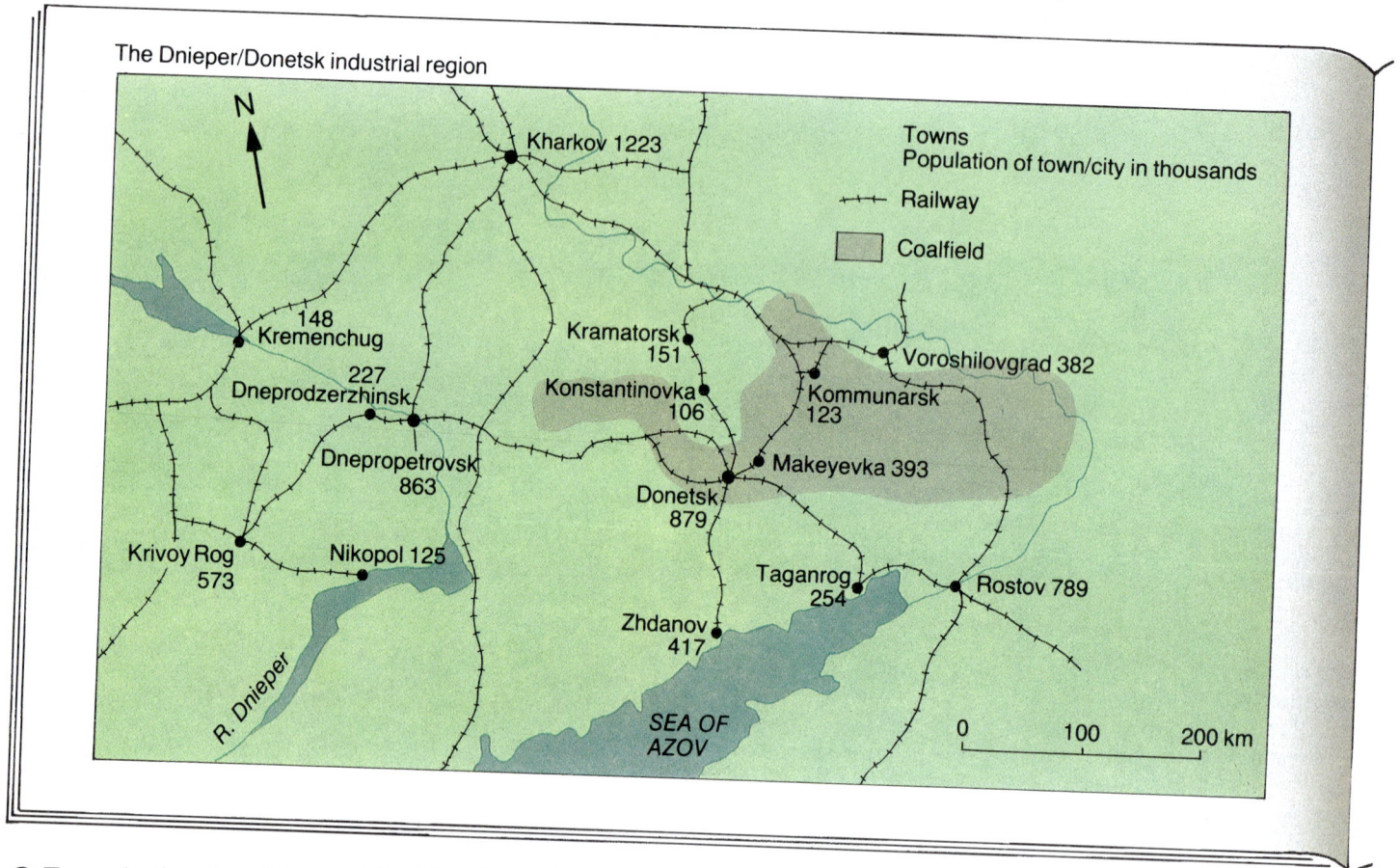

The Dnieper/Donetsk industrial region

N

Kharkov 1223

Towns
Population of town/city in thousands

⊢—⊢ Railway

Coalfield

148
Kremenchug

Kramatorsk
151

Voroshilovgrad 382

227
Dneprodzerzhinsk

Konstantinovka
106

Kommunarsk
123

Dnepropetrovsk
863

Makeyevka 393

Donetsk
879

Krivoy Rog
573

Nikopol 125

Taganrog
254

Rostov 789

Zhdanov
417

R. Dnieper

SEA OF
AZOV

0   100   200 km

❶ Test whether the statement that 'the largest towns have the most rail links' is true. Join with a friend and, from the map above, compare the size of the towns (population) and the number of rail links they have.

To do this :

ⓐ Make a list of the towns in rank order: that is from the largest to the smallest, writing them underneath each other. You can use the population figures to find the size.

ⓑ Then count how many rail links there are to each town and write another list, next to the first, with the town with the largest number of links at the top, in rank order. If two towns have the same number of rail links put them in the same order as in the first list. Your lists will begin like this:

Rank order size (population)	Rank order rail links
Kharkov (1 223)	Kharkov (6)
Donetsk (879)	Donetsk (6)
Dnepropetrovsk (863)	Rostov (4)
Rostov (789)	Krivoy Rog (4)

ⓒ Join each place with the same name in each list with a straight line like this:

Rank order size (population)	Rank order rail links
Kharkov (1 223)	Kharkov (6)
Donetsk (879)	Donetsk (6)
Dnepropetrovsk (863)	Rostov (4)
Rostov (789)	Krivoy Rog (4)

ⓓ How many times do the lines cross? Does it prove the case that the larger towns have the most rail links? Check with the list below:
- less than 5 times – statement proved
- 5 – 10 times – statement mostly correct
- 10 – 15 times – some truth in the statement
- more than 15 times – no truth in the statement.

ⓔ What did your result show?

The Azovstal metallurgical works, one of Europe's largest producers of pig iron, steel beams, bars and rails.

A china factory

The Dnieper–Donetsk industrial region

The Dnieper–Donetsk industrial region is one of the largest and most important in the USSR.

The area is heavily built up with 71% of the population living in urban areas. A dense rail and road NETWORK is used to transport the raw materials and finished products.

Coal and iron ore are the two main minerals mined in the area and it was these which attracted John Hughes. Today a range of other mining takes place for manganese, mercury, salt, clay, graphite, bauxite and for natural gas.

Such a wide range of minerals has led to a variety of industries, particularly iron and steel and machine building and metal working. The chemical industry uses the BY-PRODUCTS of these industries. There is also a large building industry.

Industries need power, and as well as coal-fired power stations energy is provided by HYDROELECTRIC power from the rivers.

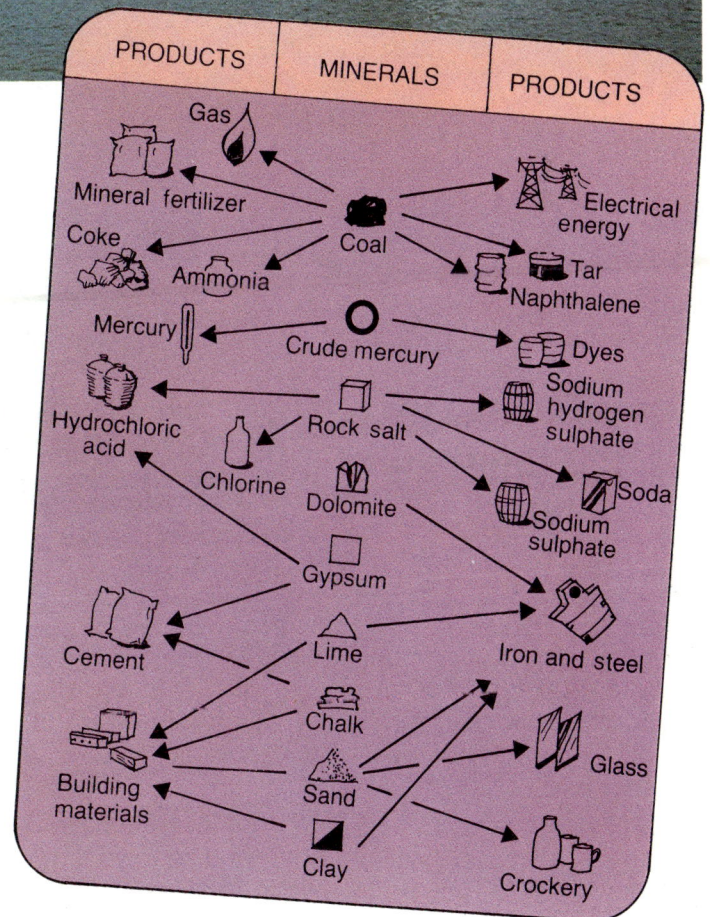

❷ Give **one** reason why:
ⓐ so many industries are found in the Dnieper–Donetsk regions;
ⓑ so many of the people live in urban areas.

❸ Look at the diagram of minerals and products. Which products need more than one mineral?

❹ Look at the photograph above of part of the Dnieper–Donetsk region. List the features shown on the photograph that you would find in any industrial region.

City of metal and coal

ДОНЕЦК

The Russian spelling of Donetsk

In the 19th century Donetsk was described like this:

'A town of weeping blast furnaces whose tears are molten metal'
'The numerous chimneys are reminiscent of a forest after a fire, with the blackened treetops still smoking'

Today, the city looks rather different:

Artyoma Street, Donetsk

Population of Donetsk	
Date	Population
1926	174 000
1939	474 000
1959	708 000
1970	880 000
1980	1 032 000
1986	1 087 000 (estimate)

❶ ⓐ On graph paper draw a line graph to show the increase in population in Donetsk: On the horizontal axis mark 1920 to 1990 with ten-year divisions every centimetre. On the vertical axis mark 11 centimetres. Each centimetre division represents 100,000 people.
ⓑ What do you notice about the population of Donetsk?

❷ What picture do the words of the 19th century writer, above, bring to your mind about the town of Donetsk?

❸ ⓐ Make a list of ten words which describe the kind of urban environment in which you would like to live. You may choose words like clean, bright and interesting.

ⓑ Now look at the photograph above of Donetsk today. Give each word in your list a mark out of 5 depending on whether the place in the photograph matches your word. Add up your scores. The best total is 50.
ⓒ Does the photograph of Donetsk show that it is a pleasant place to live?
ⓓ Do you think all of Donetsk is like this? Give a reason for your answer.

❹ ⓐ Would you change any of the words you chose for question 3a to describe the inside of the building in which you would like to work? Make the changes if you answered 'yes'.
ⓑ Give each word a score of 5 depending on whether your classroom matches your words. What was the score?
ⓒ How would you improve the environment in which you work?

The Centre of Donetsk

The map below is of the centre of the city. Artyoma is the main street with buildings like the Town Hall, local Party Committee buildings as well as the polytechnic, hotels, shops and cafés.

Many parks and gardens are found in Donetsk: The city takes great pride in its flower displays. The centre is surrounded by residential SUBURBS each with its own schools and shops. Already the suburbs of Donetsk have grown to meet those of Makeyevka, the nearest large town.

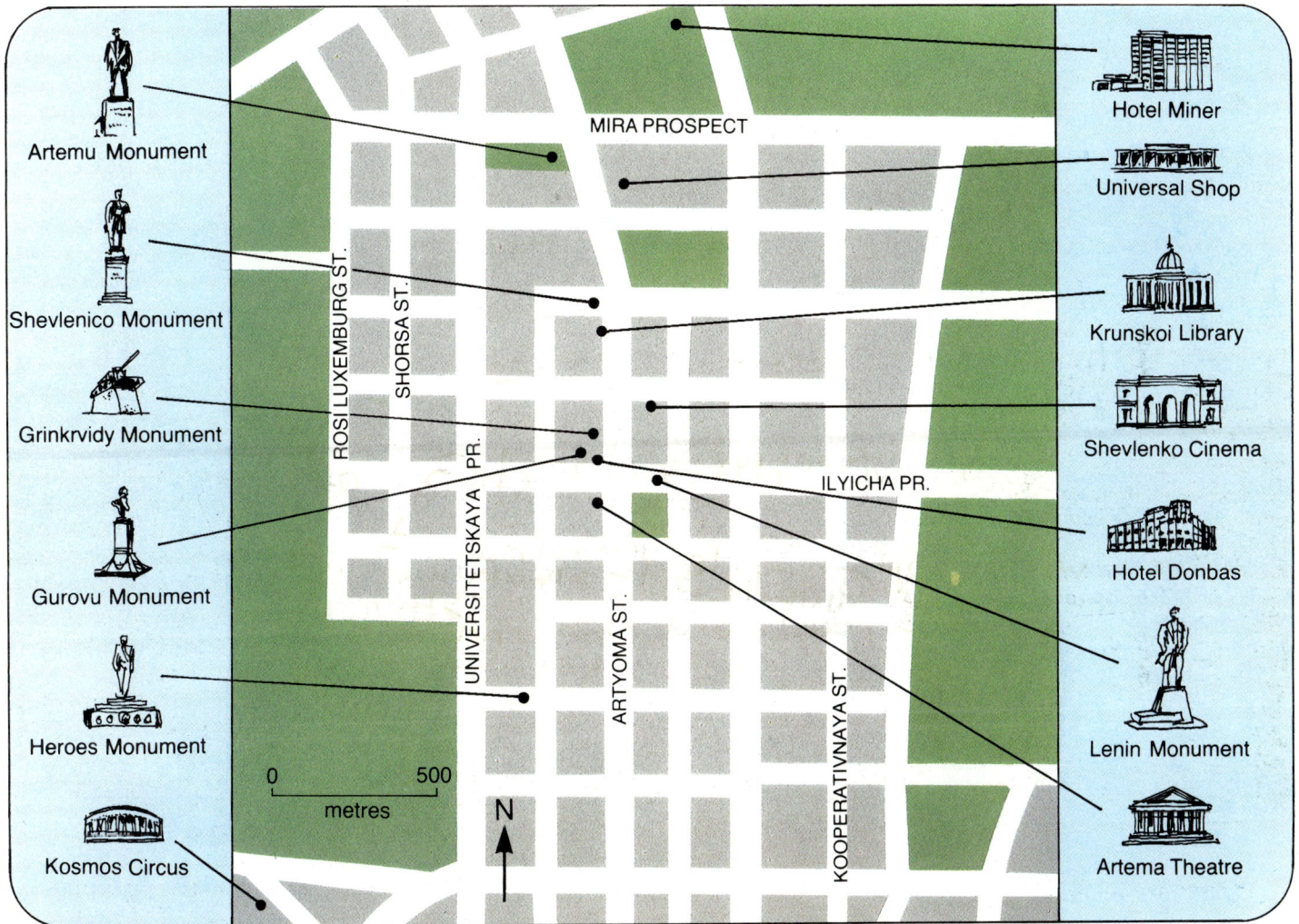

Artemu Monument

Shevlenico Monument

Grinkrvidy Monument

Gurovu Monument

Heroes Monument

Kosmos Circus

ROSI LUXEMBURG ST.

SHORSA ST.

UNIVERSITETSKAYA PR.

ARTYOMA ST.

KOOPERATIVNAYA ST.

MIRA PROSPECT

ILYICHA PR.

0   500
metres

N

Hotel Miner

Universal Shop

Krunskoi Library

Shevlenko Cinema

Hotel Donbas

Lenin Monument

Artema Theatre

❺ What two main features of the town centre do you notice when you look at the map?

❻ ⓐ Suggest an advantage of having straight streets meeting at right angles.
ⓑ Suggest a disadvantage of such a street layout.

❼ ⓐ What features have been used to try to make the city centre attractive?
ⓑ How is the city centre similar to that of your town?

❽ Join with a friend.
ⓐ Write down as many reasons as you can for making a city environment attractive.
ⓑ Write down as many ways as you can for making a city attractive.
ⓒ Make a diagram, drawing, or model of part of your ideal city.

Why not investigate?

Choose a firm in your local area and find out why it is located at its present site. You could:
■ draw a sketch map to show the position of the firm;
■ try to discover when and why the firm located at the site;
■ find out what the area was like 100 years ago;
■ draw a sketch of the firm and its surroundings to show the environment, labelling any notable features. You could then display your work and discuss it with other members of the class.

6 COMING AND GOING

In countries where there is little choice of work, people may decide to EMIGRATE in the hope of improving their lives. Some may return home at a later date. How do these movements affect the people and the countries involved?

The valley in the *Leiria* district of Portugal where the Gonzalez family lives

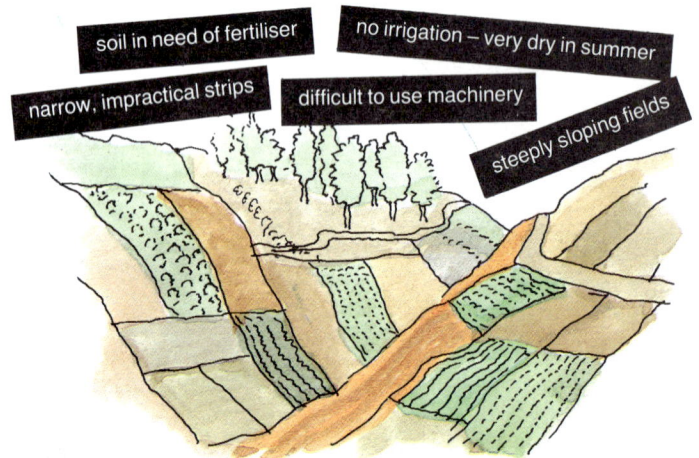

The Gonzalez family
Maria, 29
Carlos, 7
Pedro, 32
Vittoria, 3

❶ Look at the photograph of the valley in which the Gonzalez family lives;
ⓐ Pick out two details which are not usually found in the UK.
ⓑ Choose the words below which best describe the village and the landscape.
ⓒ Name at least two countries in Europe where similar scenery is found.

poor   cold   rocky   busy
dry   sunny   deserted   fertile

soil in need of fertiliser
no irrigation – very dry in summer
narrow, impractical strips
difficult to use machinery
steeply sloping fields

Problems of farming in Mediterranean regions

❷ Study the photograph and sketch above and the table of crop yields on the next page.
ⓐ Do you think it would be easy or hard to make a living here? Explain your answer carefully.
ⓑ Look at the sketch above. If you were a farmer and had the money, what changes would you make to improve the land? Trace the outline of the valley and label it with the improvements you would make.

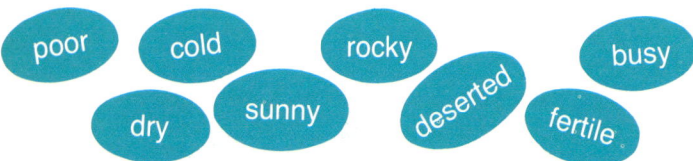

In 1970 Pedro Gonzalez and his family were thinking of moving from their farm in Portugal to France.

❸ Study the bar chart below and then copy and complete the following sentences.

ⓐ Farming employs ____% of all workers in Portugal, and of those that MIGRATE ____% are farmers.

ⓑ About 26% of migrants work in the _____ trade, though it only employs ____% of Portuguese workers as a whole.

❹ ⓐ Copy the table 'Births and deaths in Portugal, 1965–1970' below. Complete it by taking away the number of births from deaths to find the natural increase in population.

ⓑ Why would you expect the population of Portugal to rise each year?

ⓒ How might migration affect the total population?

❺ *How might the sale of farms as holiday homes affect Portuguese villages?*

❻ ⓐ How far is it from Lisbon to Paris?

ⓑ Which direction do you travel in from Paris to Lisbon?

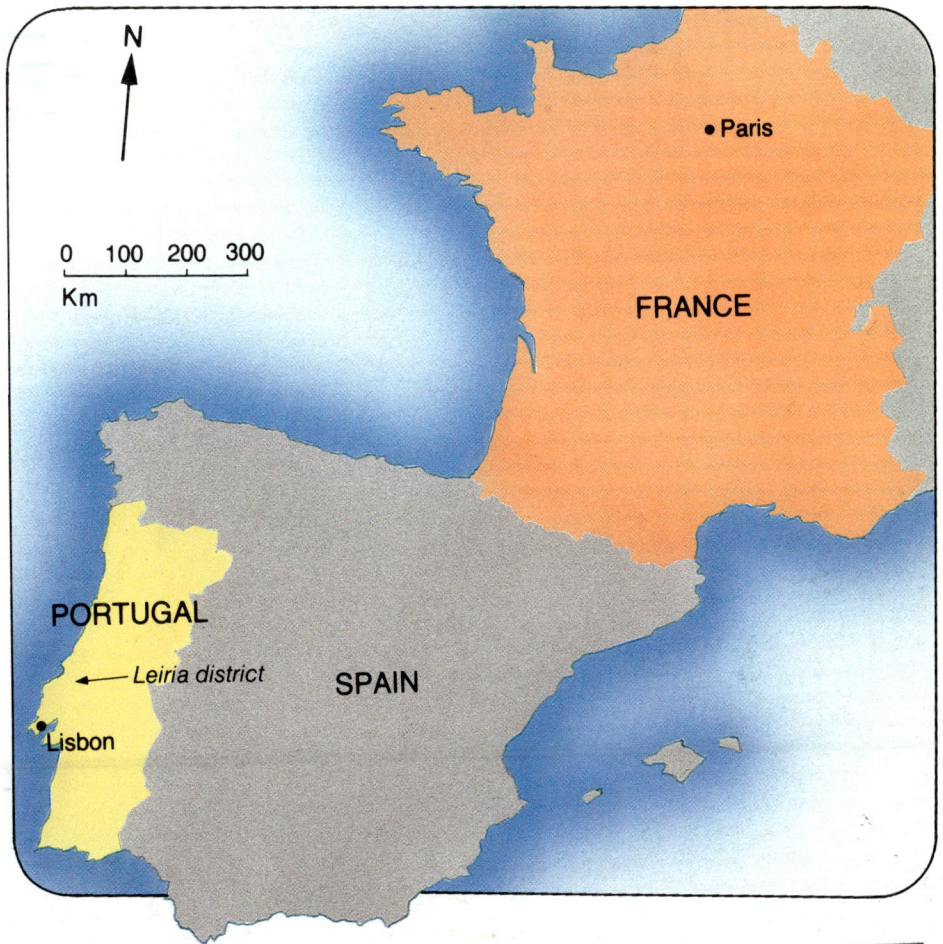

N

Paris

0   100   200   300
Km

FRANCE

PORTUGAL

← Leiria district

SPAIN

● Lisbon

EUROPEAN STATISTICAL REVIEW – PORTUGAL 1970

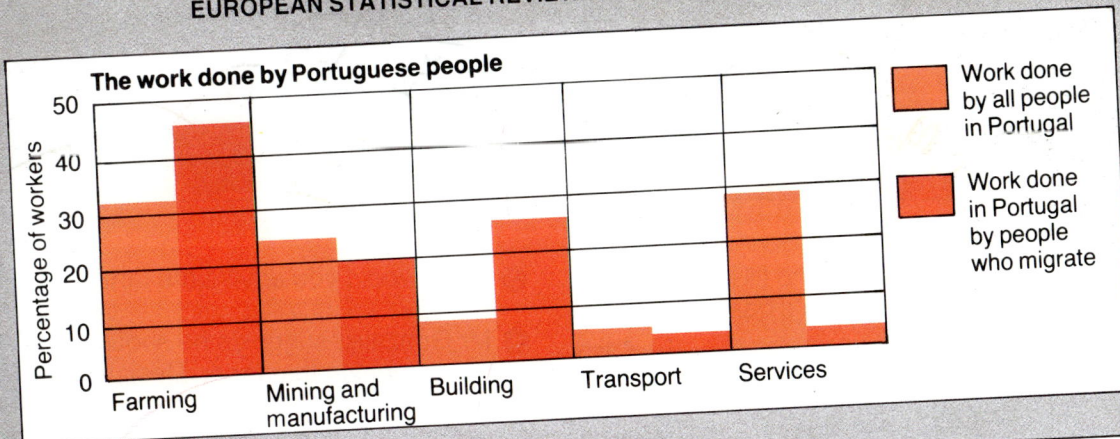

The work done by Portuguese people

Percentage of workers

Farming | Mining and manufacturing | Building | Transport | Services

■ Work done by all people in Portugal

■ Work done in Portugal by people who migrate

Births and deaths in Portugal, 1965–70 (thousands)

Year	1965	1970
Births	210	173
Deaths	95	93
Natural increase in population		

How crop yields compare

Crop	EEC (average)	Italy	Portugal
Wheat	100	70	23
Barley	100	67	15
Potatoes	100	64	35

Portugal 1970 – a family debate

Pedro: *I can no longer earn enough as a farmer although I work hard. I think we should go to France where there are more jobs. The wages are much higher too. Both my father and grandfather went to work in Brazil when they were young and they became much better off. I think I should answer an advertisement in the paper for work in France.*

Maria: *I am not so sure. We don't speak French or know anyone in France. We'd have to find a place to live and Carlos has just settled into school. It would be difficult for him. The weather would be much colder too. And what about my mother? She needs all the help we can give her.*

Pablo (Pedro's brother): *Perhaps it would help us both if you went to France. You could send money back and I could farm your land as well as mine. Our two farms together would make more money.*

Maria's mother: *Don't let me stop you going, but think carefully. The children will lose their roots; they'll never feel truly Portuguese again. There is the money but you must also consider all the things that you'll lose.*

❶ Draw a table like the one below and fill in the views of each member of the family. Pedro's has been started for you.

Name	Reasons for moving to France	Reasons for staying in Portugal
Pedro	More jobs in France, better pay ...	

❷ Decide which is the strongest argument for leaving Portugal and which is the strongest for staying. Give reasons for your choice in each case.

❸ What would you advise the family to do? Why?

❹ Mr Gonzalez suggests he should answer an advertisement in the paper. Design an advertisement to attract workers to a French car factory. Your design should emphasise: .
* GOOD PAY AND CONDITIONS
* HOLIDAYS WITH PAY * HOUSING PROVIDED
* SKILLS NOT NECESSARY * TRAINING GIVEN

❺ Use the information given in the table in the statistical review opposite to draw a bar chart. Shade the bars for people from European countries in one colour and bars for people from North African countries in another colour. Add a key.

3 months later

13 F Rue Popincourt
Paris 10
29th September 1970

Dear Mama,
We've been here six weeks now and I've only just found time to write.

Pedro didn't get the job in the car factory. There were so many better qualified people that he didn't stand a chance. However, he now has a job on a building site. It is hard work with long hours, but at least there is money coming in.

When we arrived we stayed with another Portuguese family for a few weeks. Luckily a flat became available nearby and we moved in straight away. The flat is very small and cold but it is better than the huts that the Algerians build for themselves on waste ground.

The children are finding it very difficult to settle down; Carlos cries each day on the way to school and Vittoria keeps asking for 'real' sun again.

Anyway, let's hope my next letter will be more cheerful. I've enclosed a photo of the flats we are living in. Love to everyone,
Maria XX

6 ⓐ Try to imagine what the move must have been like for Carlos and Vittoria. What sort of things would they have found different? Write a short description of their first few days in Paris.
ⓑ Do you know anyone who has moved from one country to another in this way? Ask them what it was like and what they found most difficult. You could tape their answers.

EUROPEAN STATISTICAL REVIEW – FRANCE 1970

People from other countries living in France, 1970	
Algeria	870 000
Portugal	840 000
Italy	565 000
Spain	550 000
Morocco	300 000
Tunisia	160 000
All nationalities	4 000 000

Age–sex pyramid of foreign residents in France

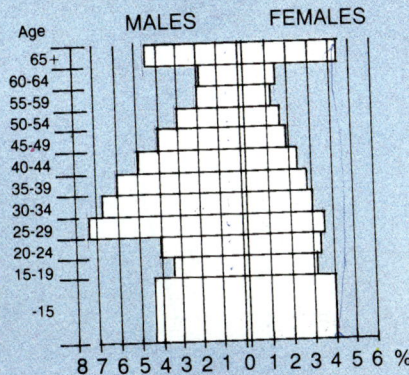

MALES   FEMALES

Age
65+
60-64
55-59
50-54
45-49
40-44
35-39
30-34
25-29
20-24
15-19
-15

8 7 6 5 4 3 2 1 0 1 2 3 4 5 6 %

7 Why do you think immigrant families often live near each other?

8 Study the age–sex pyramid on the right and then copy and complete the following sentences.

The biggest group of foreign residents in France is aged between ____ and ____ . In this group males make up ____% of the foreign population and females ____% .

9 Why are there more men than women?

24 Rue de la Convention, Paris 15
20 August 1980

Dear Pablo,

I am working in a car factory on the assembly line. The work is easier than the building site but rather boring. I don't know how long it will last as people are being made redundant. Still, I send home 350 francs a month and I've got money saved in Portugal.

Maria got a job as a waitress and with the extra money we were able to move to a better flat. Maria worries about the hostility to foreign workers in France: we are resented for having jobs when so many French people are unemployed. The government is offering a payment of 1000 francs to all immigrant workers who return home. We are thinking of leaving but the children are so well settled – it would be hard for them.

Vittoria is 13 and speaks excellent French. Carlos is about to leave school. I don't think his results will be good but he loves Paris.

I've enclosed a photo of the factory where I work and also an article from a Portuguese newsletter to give you some idea of our worries.

Love to all the family,
Pedro

❶ What changes have taken place in the lives of the Gonzalez family between 1970 and 1980? (It might help to compare Pedro's letter with Maria's on the previous page.)

❷ ⓐ Why do you think foreign workers are increasingly unwelcome in France?
ⓑ Do migrant workers do the 'dirty jobs'? Look at the tables on the right-hand page and decide whether this is true.

WHAT PRICE FOREIGN WORKERS?

The past month has shown a series of shooting attacks on immigrants and a tear gas assault on a block of flats occupied mainly by Turks. Extremists say that if France booted out its 2 million immigrant workers, unemployment would disappear. They ignore the fact that most immigrants take the dirty, poorly paid jobs that the French will not do.

EUROPEAN STATISTICAL REVIEW – FRANCE

UNEMPLOYMENT AND IMMIGRATION

Year	1970	1971	1972	1973	1974	1975	1976	1977	1978	1979	1980
Percentage unemployed	2.4	2.7	3.0	2.9	3.0	4.0	4.4	5.0	5.8	6.0	7.2
Net immigration to France	180 000	143 000	102 000	106 000	30 000	25 000	0*	0*	0*	0*	0*

* Official figures

WORK DONE BY PORTUGUESE WORKERS IN FRANCE

Farming	10%
Building	40%
Car making	20%
Catering (hotels, cafés)	15%

STATUS OF PORTUGUESE WORKERS IN FRANCE

Labourers	48%
Specialised workers	31%
Skilled workers	21%
Managers	0%

AVERAGE WAGES EARNED BY MIGRANT WORKERS IN FRANCE (francs per month)

Algerian	870
Italian	1040
Portuguese	1115
Spanish	1150
All French workers	1570

MONEY SENT HOME BY MIGRANT WORKERS IN A YEAR (million francs)

Italy	380
Portugal	850
Spain	1,100
Algeria	1,100

❸ ⓐ Make a larger copy of the grid at the bottom of the page.
ⓑ On the grid, plot line graphs to show the figures for unemployment and for migrants to France between 1970 and 1980. The figures are given in the table at the top of the page. Label each line carefully.

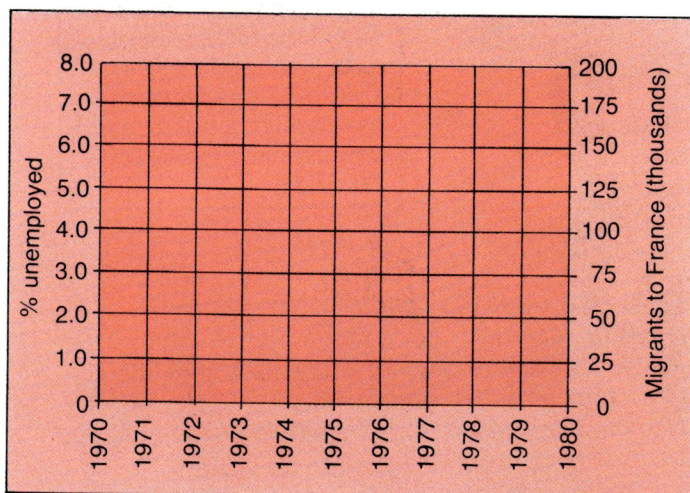

ⓒ From the following sentences write down those which you think are correct.
☐ Between 1970 and 1980, unemployment in France rose and migration to France fell.
☐ After 1975, France sent all foreign migrants home.
☐ After 1970, fewer migrants went to France as there was less chance of a job.

❹ Why do you think the wages paid to migrants are below the average paid to all French workers?

❺ *Do you think France treated its immigrants fairly? Explain your answer.*

❻ The Gonzalez family have to consider whether to stay in France or whether to return to Portugal.
ⓐ On a page of your exercise book, draw a table with two columns. Head the left-hand column *Reasons for Staying* and the right-hand column *Reasons for Leaving*. Read Pedro's letter on the previous page again and then fill in the columns.
ⓑ What would your advice be? What would your main reason be for giving this advice?

Portugal 1980 – returning

Pedro: We have returned to the village we left ten years ago. With the money we sent home we had a lovely house built – one of the best in the village. I have a new Renault car. I still have money in the bank so I may open a shop or some other business. I don't want to be a farmer again.

Maria: Isn't it a lovely house? It's what I always dreamed of when things were difficult in France. You should see the new furniture and washing machine and TV. It's just like a French home. I miss my work though. I miss meeting people every day.

Carlos: I wanted to come back but now I'm not so sure. There is no more chance to work here than in France, unless I farm with my uncle. I have no skills for another job.

Vittoria: I hate it here. I don't find it easy to speak Portuguese all the time, and I can't read or write it. It's too quiet. There is no life here – no discos, no cinema, no shops. It's so slow.

Pablo: The farm is much better now. I can make a living from it. With the money that Pedro has provided I have bought a tractor and I now use more fertiliser than I did.

❶ Was it worth it? Do you think:
ⓐ Maria and Pedro,
ⓑ Carlo and Vittoria,
ⓒ Pablo
thought the migration had been worthwhile? Give your reasons.

❷ ⓐ *How does the country which migrants leave (i) lose and (ii) gain?*
ⓑ *How does the country which migrants move to (i) lose and (ii) gain?*
Use the information from the whole unit to help you.

48

RETURNING MIGRANTS BRING NO GOOD TO US

A row has broken out in the Leiria district, north of Lisbon. A local mayor, Mr Leon Francisco has attacked the migrants who return from France and other countries and settle in the area.

Many returned migrants put their money into businesses near the coast where trade is better

'It is scandalous', he said. 'They left here ten or more years ago to get rich by working in factories in France. They abandoned their land, allowed their houses to fall into ruins and spoiled the livelihood of local traders.

But what happens when they return? Do they repair their old houses and improve their land? They do not. They are too selfish and vain for that. They have grand houses built on the edge of the village. We call them 'casa francesca' (in English, this means 'French houses'). They fill them with expensive equipment which they saw in French houses. You would think they were very superior. And how did they earn their money? By doing the dirty, boring jobs that the French workers wouldn't do.'

A farmer I spoke to said he hadn't been helped by their return. 'They don't buy food from me', he said. 'They want imported food.'

Another villager told me that some had bought local businesses, such as cafés and shops. Others preferred businesses near the coast where trade was better. I asked if they returned with useful skills. 'Not really', he replied. He added that it was the banks who gained most from the return of migrant workers. They handled the money which was sent or brought home.

❸ The newspaper article upset returned migrants. They protested. As a result a TV news team was sent to the area to make a report. They interviewed the Gonzalez family.
  Form groups of six and discuss:
● Which scenes the camera crews would film in the village.
● What questions the TV reporter would ask the Gonzalez family.
● How you think the Gonzalez family would reply.

❹ Either write a transcript of the news item or act out the interview for the rest of the class. If you have a video camera in school, film the interview. Use information from the whole unit to help you.

7 DO WE STAY OR GO?

Many people live and work in parts of the world where NATURAL DISASTERS are known to occur. Why are they prepared to settle and remain in areas which are known to be dangerous?

A TRAIL OF DISASTER AS CYCLONE STRIKES GANGES DELTA

From our Special Correspondent, John Davies.

I have just returned to Dhaka, the capital of Bangladesh, after a visit to the Ganges Delta, which was struck last night by a dreadful cyclone.

Cyclones occur in the delta every year but this was one of the worst. A wall of water up to nine metres high swept over the islands and low-lying land causing terrible damage and loss of life.

The death toll was appalling. After the water went down, people and cattle could be seen lying in the mud. Some were washed out to sea. Others were found miles inland.

Some were luckier. They told me that in places the water rose only gradually and they were able to scramble onto roofs of houses or to climb trees. But even for them the house might have given way or they may have been unable to keep grip on the slippery branches in the fierce winds.

Typical of the survivors was a young married couple, Asad and Hazera Malek. As they looked out over the desolate scene Asad told me, 'We came to this small empty island a year ago to farm the land which no one else was using. The land belongs to the government but they've never done anything with it. We grew good crops.' 'But the cyclone destroyed everything', said Hazera. 'Our home, our land, they have gone. We only escaped because we heard the warnings on a neighbour's radio just in time. Many people received no warning at all, or heard so late they would never have been able to leave the delta in time.'

Help was slow to arrive. Downpours of rain had caused serious flooding inland. Bridges collapsed, roads and railways were blocked.

Power and water supplies were affected. Medical teams were delayed.

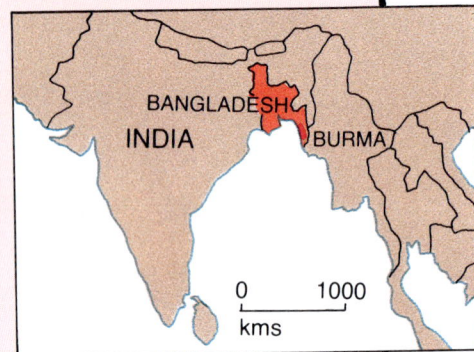

Flooding in the Ganges Delta

❶ From the newspaper article above, list the effects of the cyclone on the Ganges Delta.

❷ Look at the photograph. Imagine that you are Hazera or Asad:
 ⓐ What would you need most urgently?
 ⓑ What would you need in the future?

What is a cyclone?

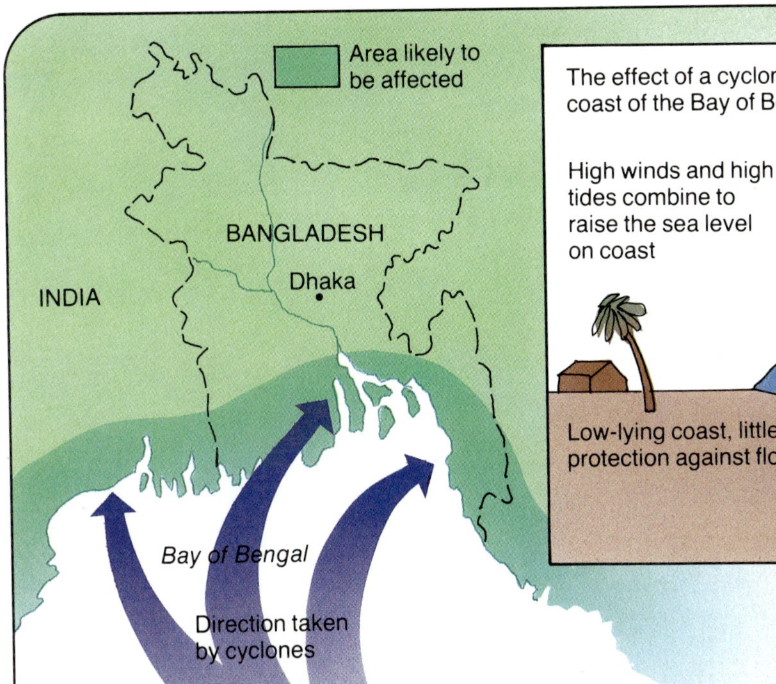

Area likely to be affected

BANGLADESH

Dhaka

INDIA

Bay of Bengal

Direction taken by cyclones

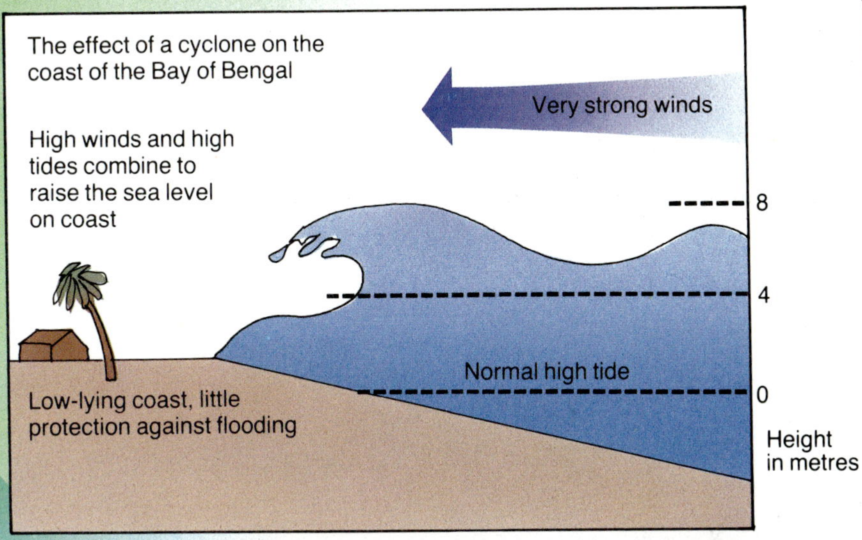

The effect of a cyclone on the coast of the Bay of Bengal

High winds and high tides combine to raise the sea level on coast

Very strong winds

Low-lying coast, little protection against flooding

Normal high tide

Height in metres

A cyclone is a violent TROPICAL storm. It is likely to occur in the Bay of Bengal in April and May, or October and November. (Similar storms would be called 'hurricanes' in the USA or 'typhoons' in South-east Asia.)

A cyclone brings torrents of rain and powerful winds up to 150 kilometres per hour. These winds can pile up water on the coast and drive enormous waves (which are called storm surges) against the coast.

If the coast is low-lying, waves of up to nine metres in height can be driven far inland. It is most dangerous if the cyclone comes at high tide.

Fortunately, cyclones are rare and most of them do not reach land. Even if they do, they soon die out over land. It is only the coastal area which is in danger.

A cyclone as seen from a satellite

❸ From the text above, state two features of a cyclone which make it so dangerous.

❹ Study the diagrams above and fill in the correct words in this paragraph:

Strong winds come from the ____ __ _____ . High winds and high _____ raise the _____ level along the coast. The height of the waves can be about ____ metres. The coast is ___ _____ and there is little protection against _____ .

❺ 'This is Radio Bangladesh. Here is a cyclone warning: A cyclone is expected to hit the coast at 1400 hours.'

ⓐ Complete the cyclone warning, describing what weather conditions it will bring and what areas will be affected.

ⓑ Discuss with a friend what things Radio Bangladesh might advise people to do and what they would advise them not to do.

ⓒ Design a poster, to be displayed in the Delta, which illustrates what people should do when a cyclone is approaching.

ⓓ Why do many people not do what the warnings suggest?

Water, water everywhere

Bangladesh is a very flat country which was formed by the huge rivers which flow through it.

BANGLADESH IS A GIANT DELTA

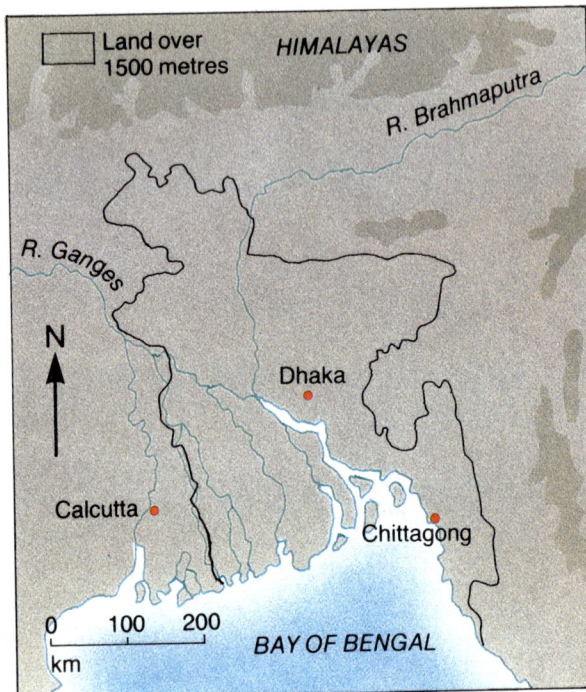

The rivers of Bangladesh

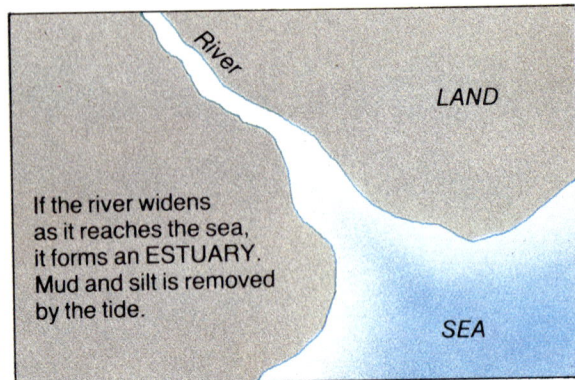

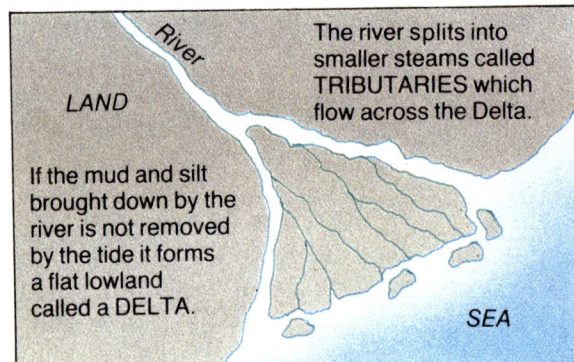

If the river widens as it reaches the sea, it forms an ESTUARY. Mud and silt is removed by the tide.

If the mud and silt brought down by the river is not removed by the tide it forms a flat lowland called a DELTA.

The river splits into smaller steams called TRIBUTARIES which flow across the Delta.

No part of Bangladesh is more than 30 metres above sea level. Most of the land has been formed by rivers which flow through it. These rivers, especially the Ganges and Brahmaputra, carry down countless tonnes of mud, sand and SILT. When they reach the sea, the rivers drop this material. The tides have not been able to remove such huge amounts of material and it has formed the land of the DELTA. New land is constantly being formed, in the first place as islands off the coast. The delta is criss-crossed by a large number of streams and rivers, some of which change course suddenly.

❶ Study the information above, then copy and complete the following:

ⓐ Bangladesh is a giant ____ which has been formed by rivers such as the _____ and the _____ . When they reach the Bay of _____, huge amounts of mud, _____ and _____ are deposited. The tide is not strong enough to _____ it away and it forms new land. As they flow across the delta the rivers split up to form _____ .

ⓑ Why do you think it is difficult to build roads and railways across Bangladesh?

ⓒ The main port of Bangladesh is Chittagong.
  (i) How far is Chittagong from Dhaka?
  (ii) Why would it be difficult to have a port on the delta?

❷ Look carefully at the shape of an estuary and a delta shown on the diagrams above. Use an atlas to find out whether the following rivers have a delta or an estuary: Mersey, Thames, Nile, Mississippi, St. Lawrence, Rhône.

Asif, a schoolboy in Dhaka writes to John his pen friend in London. Here is an extract from his letter:

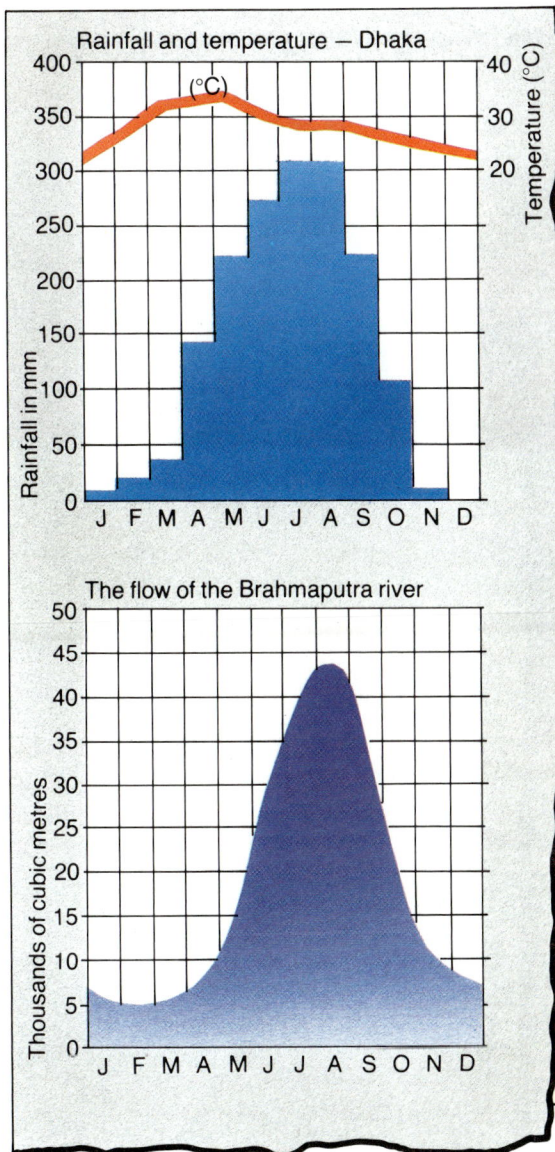

Rainfall and temperature — Dhaka

The flow of the Brahmaputra river

It is the wet season now and the rain comes down in torrents. It hardly seems to stop for days on end. The air is always damp and mould grows on everthing, even my sandals which I take off at night. It will be cooler and drier in the winter. The rains are not reliable though. In one year the rainfall will be low and then the rice crop is poor. In another the rains are so heavy that the summer rice crop cannot be harvested or the autumn crop planted.

With the rain, the floods come. The heavy rain and the snow melting in the Himalayas cause the great rivers to swell. They are up to 3 miles wide in the delta and about 1/3 of the country may be flooded. We need the floods. They bring water for our crops and they drop silt which makes the soil fertile. I am enclosing some graphs which I found in a magazine. Perhaps they will help you understand better.

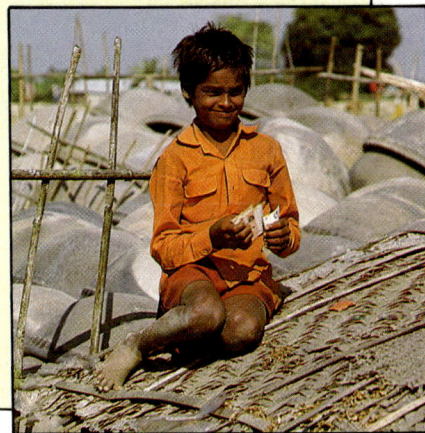

Asif

Rainfall and temperature – London

Month	J	F	M	A	M	J	J	A	S	O	N	D
Rainfall (mm)	48	40	50	45	48	52	60	56	49	65	55	57
Temperature (°C)	5	7	8	10	13	16	18	16	15	10	6	5

❸ Study the rainfall and temperature graph for Dhaka above.
ⓐ What is the rainfall and temperature in April?
ⓑ Compare the weather in July and December.
ⓒ The table above shows the rainfall and temperature in London. Draw a bar graph to show rainfall and a line graph to show temperature. Use a similar scale to one in the Dhaka graph above.

❹ Write part of a letter from John to Asif in which he describes the weather in London and points out the ways in which it is different from Dhaka.

❺ ⓐ Reading from the graph above, state the flow of the River Brahmaputra in (i) May and (ii) August.
ⓑ The Thames in London is less likely to flood. Explain why.

The people

Bangladesh is a poor, very crowded country. It has to feed more and more people each year.

Children being vaccinated in a clinic

FACT SHEET

★ Every year about 4 million babies are born in Bangladesh
★ Each child has a 1 in 8 chance of dying before its first birthday and a 1 in 4 chance of dying before it is 5.
★ The most likely cause of death is MALNUTRITION. About half the population is permanently underfed.
★ Death may result from dysentery, whooping cough or measles.
★ There is only one doctor for every 10 000 people and one hospital bed for every 6 000 people.
★ A person in Bangladesh lives, on average, until the age of 46.

Bangladesh – population details

Year	Total population (millions)	Density (per sq km)	BIRTH RATE (per 1000)	DEATH RATE (per 1000)	NATURAL % INCREASE
1971	69	483	—	—	—
1973	72	501	—	—	—
1976	77	533	50	28	2.2
1979	85	588	47	21	2.6
1982	93	643	47	19	2.8
1985	101	706	45	17	2.8

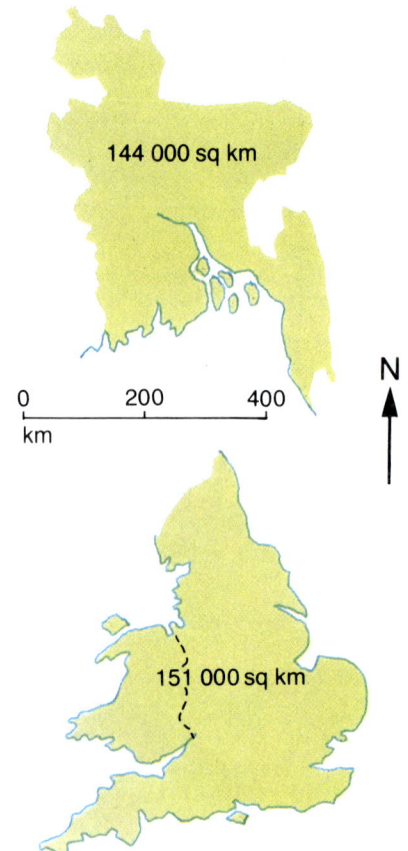

144 000 sq km

151 000 sq km

0   200   400
km

N

❶ Look at the table above and then:
ⓐ Draw a line graph to show the changes in total population in Bangladesh between 1971 and 1985.
ⓑ How has the change in total population affected the DENSITY of population?

❷ ⓐ Trace the maps of Bangladesh and of England and Wales. Place 101 dots on the map of Bangladesh to show its population of 101 million. Place 50 dots in England and Wales to show its 50 million people.
ⓑ Write a sentence to compare the population density of the two areas.

❸ Look at the fact sheet above:
ⓐ Suggest three reasons why people in Bangladesh are likely to die at an early age.
ⓑ Look at the death rate. Why do you think it is now falling?

Making a living

Many people try to make a living in a dangerous area because there is little alternative.

Employment

Pie charts for Bangladesh and United Kingdom

- Industry
- Agriculture
- Services

My father was a sharecropper. He grew crops on a hectare of land and he had to pay a half share of his crop to the landlord for rent. The other half was used to feed the family, to provide seed for next year and to sell so he could pay taxes, buy fertiliser and meet general expenses.

My father was a landless labourer. When my grandfather died his land was divided amongst all the sons. They all got a tiny amount so father sold his share to his eldest brother. Each day after that he left the house to look for work. If he was lucky he could buy 2 lbs of rice with his day's wages. On many days there was no work.

Asad and Hazera Malek describe their fathers' work.

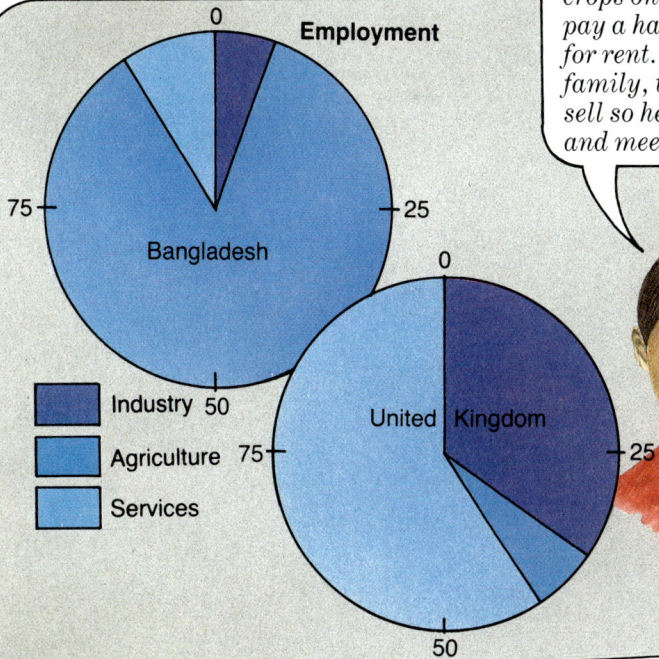

JUTE

One of the few crops which can be grown in Bangladesh and sold abroad is **Jute**. It is like giant rhubarb and grows two metres high. But the crop is not for eating. From its stalk comes a coarse fibre which can be made into a cloth for making sacks or the back of linoleum. This is done in large jute mills.

Bangladesh used to sell a lot to Britain. But not any more. There are too many things that can be used instead for sacks and linoleum. Also Britain charges high taxes on jute products from abroad in order to protect her own jute factories in Dundee.

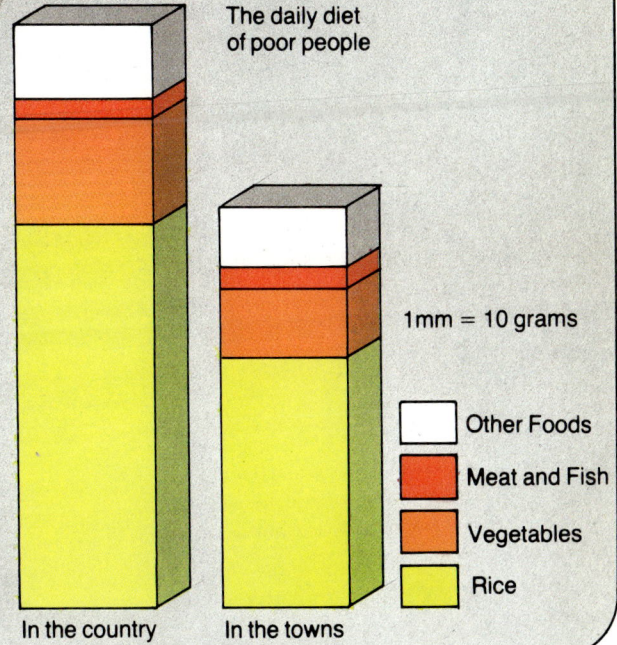

The daily diet of poor people

1mm = 10 grams

- Other Foods
- Meat and Fish
- Vegetables
- Rice

In the country   In the towns

❹ Copy and complete the table below to compare how people are employed in Bangladesh and in the UK.

Percentage employed in:	Bangladesh	United Kingdom
Industry		
Agriculture		
Services		
TOTAL		

ⓐ Describe the differences shown by the pie charts above and your table.

❺ Read Asad's and Hazera's comments above.
ⓐ What is the difference between a 'sharecropper' and a 'landless labourer'?
ⓑ Which one do you think is better off? Explain why?

❻ Read the section on jute. Why is there little chance of more jobs in the jute mills in Bangladesh?

❼ Look at the daily diet of poor people in the countryside and in the towns.
ⓐ In what ways are the diets similar?
ⓑ In what ways are they different?
ⓒ Can you think of any reasons for the differences?

❽ *What would be the advantages of cultivating new land in the delta?*

What shall we do?

Asad and Hazera must now decide where they will go to try to earn a living. Should they leave Bangladesh and go to:

LONDON?

HAZERA: *I suggest we go to London if we can because my sister is already there. We could stay with her.*

ASAD: *What would we do there? It is difficult to find work in London.*

HAZERA: *We could help my sister and her husband in their shop. They sell food to other Bangladeshi people who live in the neighbourhood. Perhaps one day we could open our own shop.*

ASAD: *It would be costly and difficult to get to London. Not many people are allowed to emigrate to the UK but we do have relatives there …*

KUWAIT?

ASAD:
I could get a job working on a building site in Kuwait for two years: building a hospital, or school or factory. I could earn five or six times as much as I could here even without any skills.

HAZERA:
But you would be away for two years. What would happen to me?

ASAD:
I would send you money. I would have to work long hours and live in a workers' camp. I could save a lot.

HAZERA:
You would need to take care. There are often accidents and you would not be looked after. I'd hate being separated for so long.

ASAD: *There seems to be little opportunity in the countryside. Perhaps we would be better in the city. Let's go to Dhaka.*

HAZERA: *But what would we do there? How would we live?*

ASAD: *There is more work in Dhaka than anywhere else. Hotels and offices want cleaners and messengers. There are factories that we could buy and sell food to.*

HAZERA: *And where would we live?*

ASAD: *We would stay with relatives for a while until we were able to find a place to build our own house.*

HAZERA: *But it's so crowded and we'd never be able to grow our own rice and vegetables. I'd also miss all the bananas and mangoes that we get in the country.*

DHAKA?

OR SHOULD THEY STAY IN THE DELTA?

❶ Use the information in this unit to decide which arguments could be put forward by Asad and Hazera for staying in, or leaving the delta.

❷ ⓐ Work in groups of about four. Write down the arguments for and against each of the four alternatives.

ⓑ Decide what is the strongest argument for and against the move in each case, in your opinion.

ⓒ Would they be the strongest arguments for Asad and Hazera? Why might there be a difference?

ⓓ What would you advise them to do? Explain your decision to the class.

Why not investigate?

Collect information about a natural disaster which has occurred recently in the world. It may be a flood, an earthquake or a volcanic eruption.

● Try to explain why the natural disaster occurred.

● Describe the effects of the disaster on the local population.

● Would you expect the local population to remain in, or return to the area? Give reasons for your answer.

0   500   1000
km

57

8 SHOULD THE DESERT BLOOM?

People may overcome the problem of living in a difficult ENVIRONMENT. This is often done at great cost. Should natural environments be preserved or changed to provide a pleasant place for people to live?

The Arizona Desert at sunrise – a view taken outside Phoenix

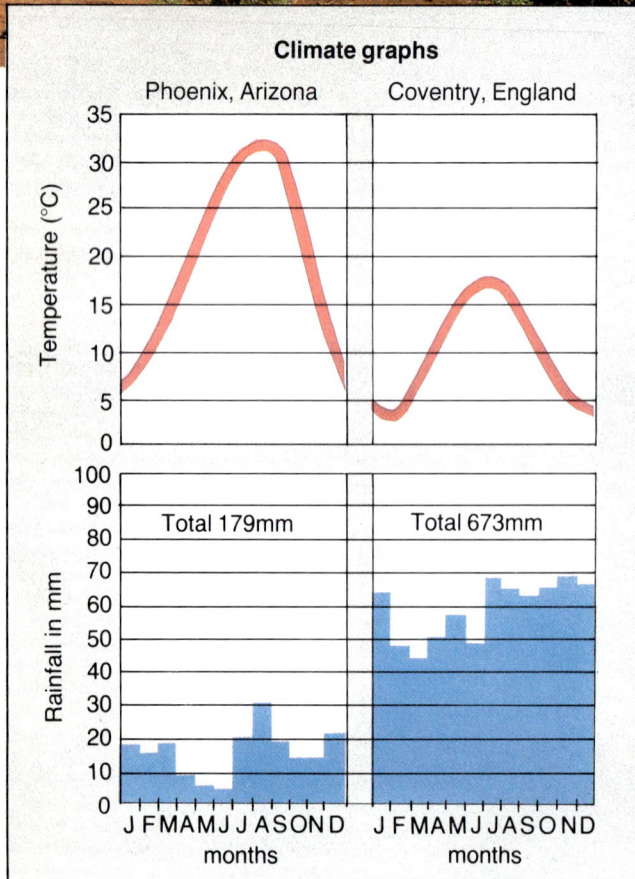

Climate graphs

Phoenix, Arizona   Coventry, England

Temperature (°C)

Total 179mm   Total 673mm

Rainfall in mm

J F M A M J J A S O N D   J F M A M J J A S O N D
months   months

❶ ⓐ Look at the photograph above and the table below. Give a score from +3 to −3 to each pair of words which best describes how you feel about the desert shown.

FRIENDLY	+3 +2 +1 0 −1 −2 −3	UNFRIENDLY
EXCITING	+3 +2 +1 0 −1 −2 −3	BORING
BEAUTIFUL	+3 +2 +1 0 −1 −2 −3	UGLY
PLEASANT	+3 +2 +1 0 −1 −2 −3	UNPLEASANT
ATTRACTIVE	+3 +2 +1 0 −1 −2 −3	UNATTRACTIVE
INTERESTING	+3 +2 +1 0 −1 −2 −3	UNINTERESTING
WELCOMING	+3 +2 +1 0 −1 −2 −3	HOSTILE

ⓑ Now write down how you feel about the picture. Compare your feelings with those of a neighbour.

❷ ⓐ Look at the climate graphs on the left and complete these sentences:
 (i) The highest monthly temperature in Phoenix is _____ .
 (ii) The lowest monthly temperature in Phoenix is _____ .
 (iii) The total rainfall in Phoenix is _____ .
ⓑ Copy out the sentences below, choosing the correct word from each bracket.
The climate in Phoenix differs from that of Coventry. In Phoenix the weather is (hotter/colder) and the rainfall is (higher/lower).

89% of Arizona State water is used by farmers.

Phoenix water customers use an average of 1230 litres of water per day. Seventy gallons are used in showers, toilets, washing machines, dishwashers and for other home uses.

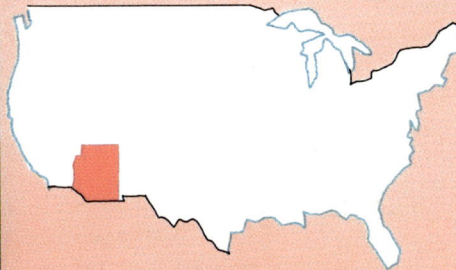

590 litres per person per day of the water in Phoenix is used for watering trees, shrubs and grass.

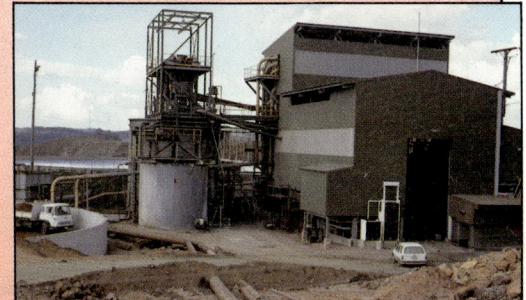

180 litres of water per person in Arizona goes to COMMERCIAL use.

A LUXURIOUS HOME AND TIME TO ENJOY IT

ARIZONA HOMES LTD

WELCOME TO THE VALLEY OF THE SUN

A	1940	1950	1960	1970	1980
Population of metropolitan Phoenix (thousands)	186	331	663	971	1508
Phoenix area (in square miles)	9.6	17.1	187.4	247.9	330.6

B		1960	1980	1982
Water connections (thousands)		122	282	298
Water production (billions of litres)		153	403	460
Wastewater connections (thousands)		90	263	270

❸ Use the following words and the climate graph of Phoenix, on the left-hand page, to design an advertisement to attract people to come and live in Arizona.
Plenty of sunshine – Outdoor leisure – 1 000 Tennis courts – All-year-round – 68 Golf courses – Swimming – Desert hiking – Horse riding – Sun shines 86% of the time.

❹ Working in pairs:
ⓐ List three reasons why people might wish to come and live in the desert.
ⓑ List the four main uses of water in Arizona.

❺ *Write down what the link is between Table **A** and Table **B** above. (You need to decide what each shows before answering.)*

THE CENTRAL ARIZONA PROJECT CANAL

THE COLORADO – RIVER OF LIFE?

The $1.6 billion Central Arizona Project Canal is nearly finished. Soon it will bring water from the Colorado across the desert to Phoenix and Tuscon. Towns, farms and industries will all be able to use the badly needed water.

The Colorado River, rising in the snow capped Rocky Mountains of Colorado, holds the key to the water supply in the southwest of the United States.

Cutting through the Grand Canyon, the river winds southwards through the desert before reaching the Gulf of California over 2 000 kilometres from its source.

The newly-built Central Arizona Project Canal will take water from the Parker Dam, 500 kilometres across the desert to cities like Phoenix and Tuscon.

The water is badly needed to supply the growing population in this part of Arizona. As the water flows along the 350 kilometre canal much of it may dry-up leaving the water tasting salty when it reaches Tuscon.

Costs have steadily increased since the Project started but by the time it is completed in 1991 its builders hope it will provide water for all who live in the Arizona Desert.

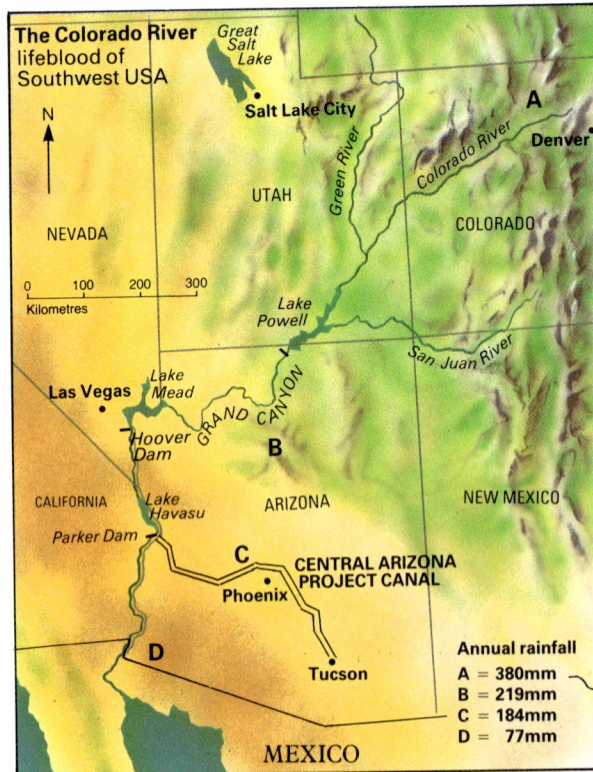

The Colorado River lifeblood of Southwest USA

Annual rainfall
A = 380mm
B = 219mm
C = 184mm
D = 77mm

The Central Arizona Project Canal snaking across the desert

❶ Look at the map and article above and complete the following:
The Central Arizona Canal crosses the desert from the _____ _____ to _____ . The canal is ___ kilometres long and brings water to the cities of _____ and _____ .

❷ From the map:
ⓐ What is the rainfall near the source of the Colorado River?
ⓑ What is the total rainfall near the mouth of the Colorado River?
ⓒ Which letter **A**, **B**, **C** or **D** on the map is furthest north?
ⓓ How do rainfall totals change from north to south along the Colorado River?

Is it worth $1.6 billion dollars?

Joe and Lesley Goldwater say.... YES!

Joe and Lesley Goldwater moved to Phoenix from Chicago when the heavy metals factory, in which they worked, closed down. They now have jobs with an electronics firm making parts for radar. The house in which they live cost them $120 000 which is above the average for the USA, but average for Phoenix.

Growing crops in the desert needs a great deal of water. Farms supply fresh vegetables and fruit to cities like Phoenix. Cotton grows well here. The desert soil is very rich and all we need are large quantities of water. The Central Arizonal Project will help agriculture.

The water is needed in Phoenix. — As the city continues to grow, new housing areas out here in the desert depend on new water supplies.
More and more people want to come to live here and enjoy what the desert has to offer. Water and wealth in this city go together.

For industry to succeed in the desert it needs water. The high technology industries of Phoenix, like computers, electronics and aerospace, all use water. The Central Arizona Project Canal will help keep the industries running and provide jobs for the people who come here.

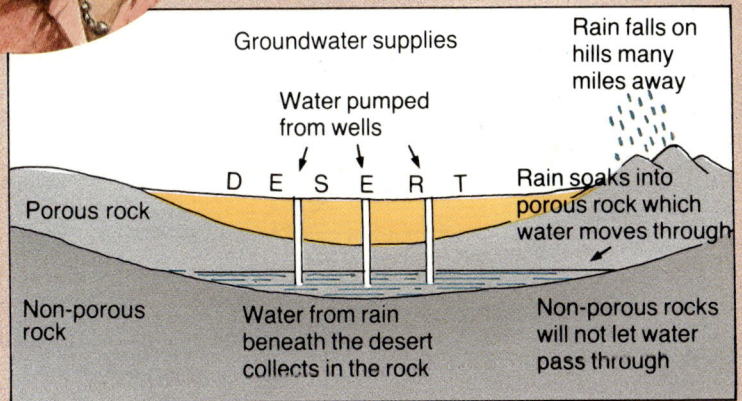

Our groundwater supplies in Arizona are getting lower every year. We need to make sure the wells don't run dry. The water from the Central Arizona Project Canal will help us keep underground water levels steady.

Groundwater supplies

Water pumped from wells

Rain falls on hills many miles away

D E S E R T

Porous rock

Rain soaks into porous rock which water moves through

Non-porous rock

Water from rain beneath the desert collects in the rock

Non-porous rocks will not let water pass through

---

3 ⓐ Why do the cities need water from the Arizona Canal Project?
ⓑ Why do the farmers need water from the Arizona Canal Project?

4 Look at the information about groundwater.
ⓐ What is groundwater?
ⓑ How does the water get underground in the desert?
ⓒ How does the water become trapped under the desert?
ⓓ How is the groundwater brought to the surface?

5 ⓐ Join with a neighbour and copy the following table. Then fill in the reasons that the Goldwater's give for so much money being spent on the Project. One reason has been filled in for you already.

YOUR REASON	SCORE	ORDER
1 The water is needed in Phoenix		
2		
3		
4		

ⓑ Give a score out of 10 for each reason, according to how important you think it is.
ⓒ Use your scores to put the reasons in order from 1 to 4.
ⓓ Explain to others in your class how you decided on your most important reason.

6 Using the information you have read so far in this unit, give as many reasons as you can why the Central Arizona Project Canal went ahead.

The River Colorado – where does all the water go?

The Grand Canyon of the Colorado is considered to be one of the wonders of the world.

The Colorado helps California to enjoy the blessing of water without the inconvenience of rain.

A desalination plant is needed because the water reaching Mexico is salty – so much has been taken and has evaporated from the large reservoir. The river almost vanishes into the sand before it reaches the sea.

8.55 = Billions of litres of water in the Colorado River

6.44

COLORADO

UTAH

12.53

11.43

NEVADA

to Las Vegas

NEW MEXICO

11.77

D E S E R T

ARIZONA

10.33

CALIFORNIA

Colorado River aqueduct (California)

8.55

Central Arizona project (Arizona)

All American canal (California)

7.04

Gila Granty main canal (Arizona)

Alamo canal

2.04

MEXICO

0

Gulf of California

400

300

200

100

0 km

The Colorado River passes through turbines to provide power.

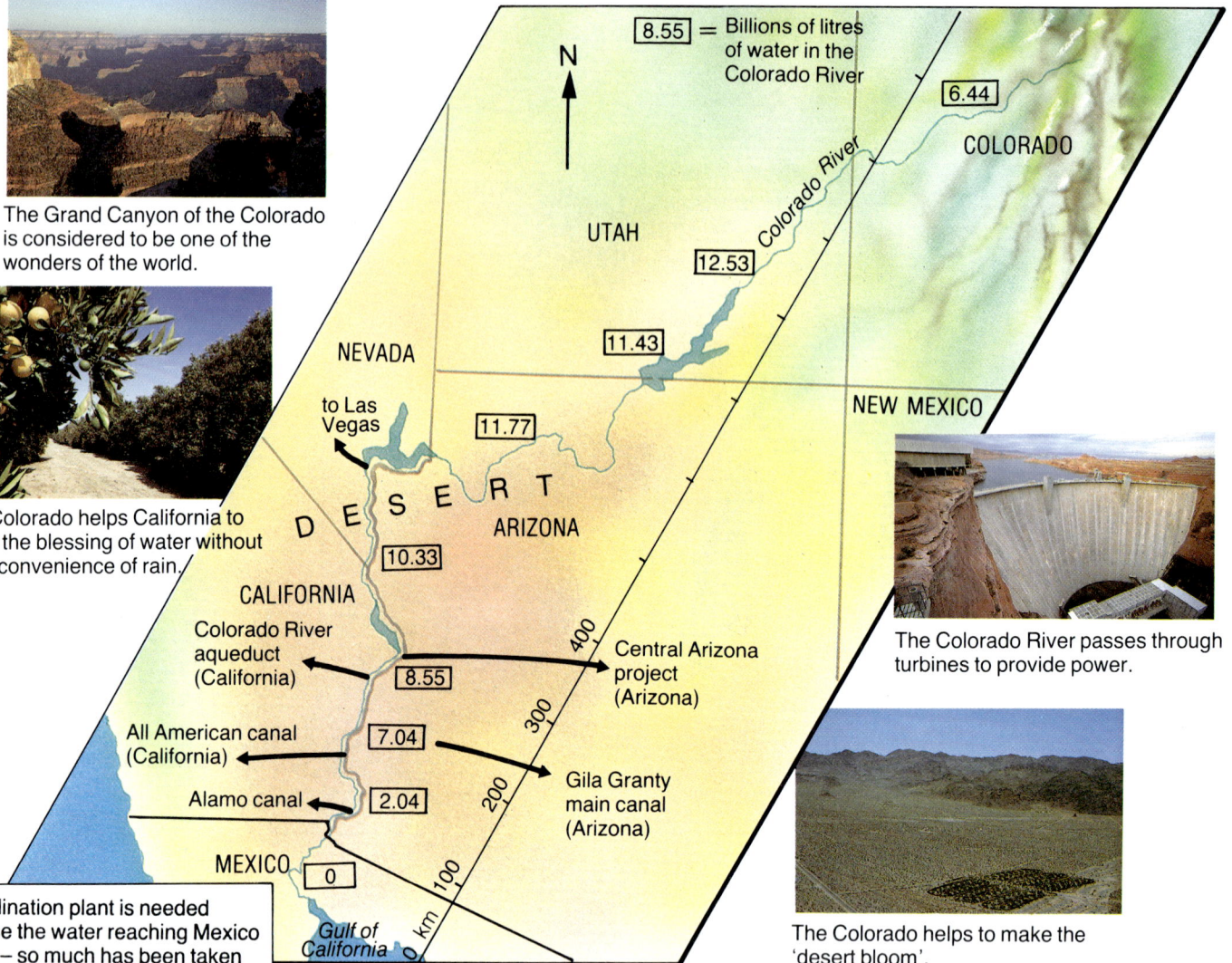
The Colorado helps to make the 'desert bloom'.

❶ ⓐ On a framework, like the one below, draw a graph (using the figures in the table on the right) to show the amount of water in the Colorado River at points from its mouth to its source. A graph for the River Thames is already shown on the framework.

ⓑ What differences does your graph show between the flow of water in the Colorado River and that of the River Thames?

ⓒ Look at the diagram above and suggest two reasons for the differences.

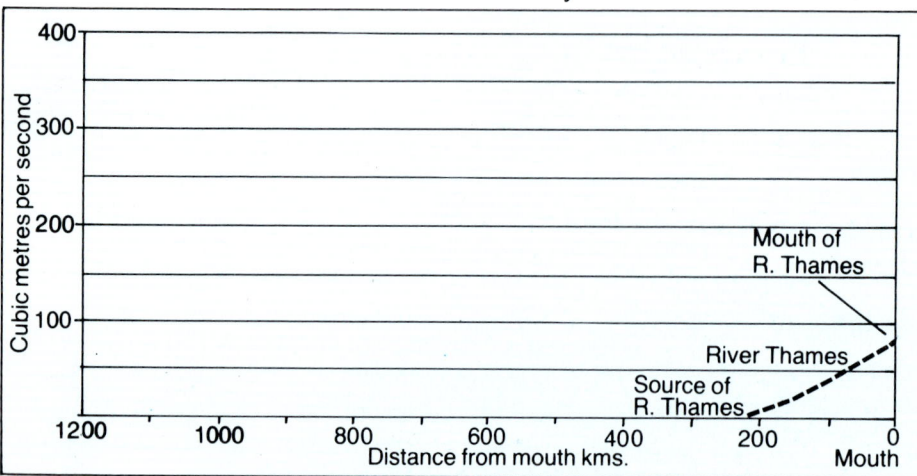

Mouth of R. Thames

River Thames

Source of R. Thames

Cubic metres per second

Distance from mouth kms. Mouth

River Thames		River Colorado	
Dist. from mouth (km)	Flow (m³ per sec)	Dist. from mouth (km)	Flow (m³ per sec)
215	3.3	1200	204.2
160	14.2	950	397.3
123	28.4	850	362.4
50	59.1	500	271.1
0	77.1	200	223.2
		100	64.7

The C.A.P. – a $1.6 billion disaster?

To provide water for the Central Arizona Project it will be necessary to build four dams to collect the water which will flow along the canal. These reservoirs will flood the land on the valley floors. This is where many birds breed including the hawk and the rare southern bald eagle. Hunting, fishing and birdwatching will be affected.

Agriculture uses 90% of the water consumed in Arizona but only produces 3% of the total income.

The Orme reservoir will flood the Apache Indian Reservation and force the people to leave their 16 000 acres of fertile lowland. They will have to settle on 2 500 acres of rocky upland.

We don't think that we really need the water at all. Wasting water is a crime now. Already conservation measures are having an effect. If our use of water is reduced we will have enough from existing supplies.

To get water from the Colorado River to Tucson means pumping it 700 metres uphill. This would take as much electricity as the city of Phoenix uses now. It would be wasteful.

All the C.A.P. is doing is supplying water so that businessmen who buy and sell land and housing get rich. Phoenix is big enough already. People keep coming because of the huge advertising campaign.

❷ Look at the arguments on this page against the Central Arizona Canal, and at the map opposite. Write down which you think are the weakest arguments given here against the scheme. Why are they weak?

❸ Decide, using the evidence on these two pages, and that given by Joe and Lesley Goldwater, whether you are for or against the scheme. Which was the most important reason which helped you decide?

❹ Join with two others and choose one of the following activities:

ⓐ Each of you take one of the following roles:
– a supporter of the Central Arizona Project;
– an ORNITHOLOGIST and NATURALIST;
– an Apache chief.

The supporter of the scheme must find reasons from this unit which will persuade each of the others that the scheme is needed. The others should be clear about why they do not want the scheme. Have a discussion and see who persuades the group that their view is right.

ⓑ Each of you take one of the following roles:
– an opponent of the Central Arizona Project;
– a farmer who wants to irrigate more of his land;
– a person who is hoping to come and live in Phoenix.

The opponent of the scheme must find reasons from this unit which will persuade each of the others that the scheme is unnecessary. The others should be clear about why they want the scheme to go ahead. Have a discussion, and see who persuades the group that their view is right.

❺ ⓐ A demonstration is to be held in Phoenix in support of your viewpoint (i.e. either that the Central Arizona Canal Project should go ahead or that it should be abandoned). Find someone who agrees with you and:

(i) write two or three slogans for the placard your supporters could carry as they take part in the demonstration;

(ii) design a poster which you could display to support your case.

ⓑ *Imagine that you are a reporter from the* Arizona Tribune *reporting on this demonstration. Write an account of what happened giving points of view for and against the scheme.*

U.S.A. water – a precious resource nationwide

Dry America

100th MERIDIAN. Historically the boundary between wet and dry America.

100°W

Missouri R.

Columbia R.

COLUMBIA RIVER
A staircase of reservoirs from Canada to its mouth.

WATER IN CALIFORNIA
California needs more water than it can supply itself. It brings water from the Colorado River through large, expensive AQUEDUCTS.

CHEYENNE
annual rainfall 376mm

SAN FRANCISCO
annual rainfall 500mm

Arkansas R.

Colorado R.

750 billion litres of water per day withdrawn from resources.
52% not returned.
48% used and returned.

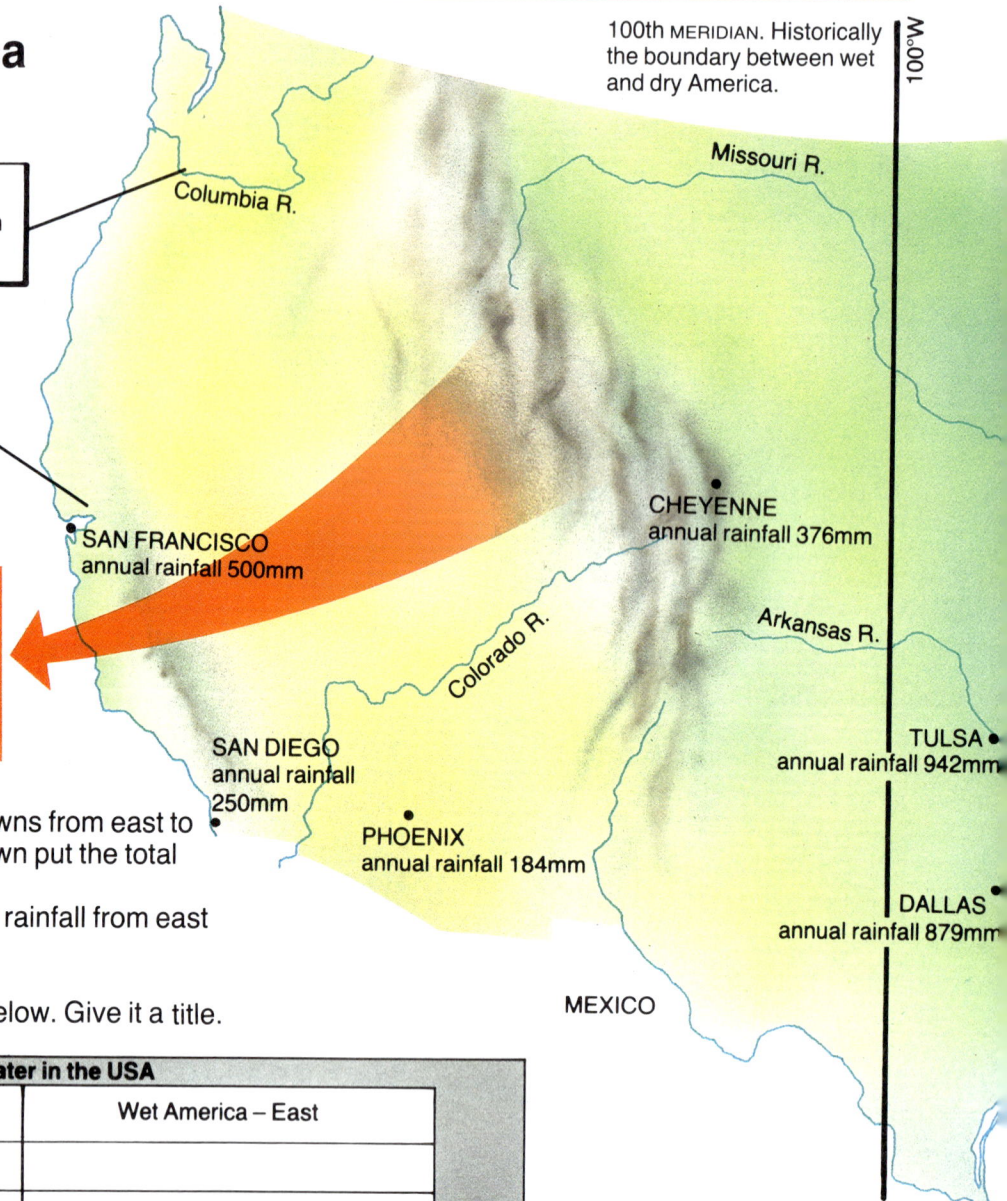

SAN DIEGO
annual rainfall 250mm

PHOENIX
annual rainfall 184mm

TULSA
annual rainfall 942mm

DALLAS
annual rainfall 879mm

MEXICO

❶ ⓐ Use the map to make a list of towns from east to west across the USA. Next to each town put the total rainfall figure.
ⓑ What do you notice about the total rainfall from east to west across the USA?

❷ ⓐ Copy and complete the graph below. Give it a title.

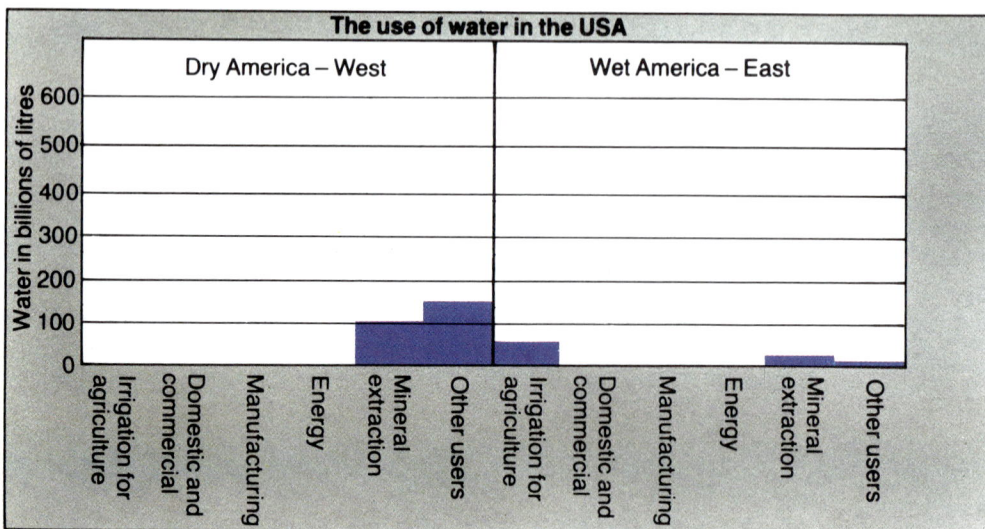

The use of water in the USA												
Dry America – West						Wet America – East						

Water in billions of litres: 600, 500, 400, 300, 200, 100, 0

Dry America – West: Irrigation for agriculture, Domestic and commercial, Manufacturing, Energy, Mineral extraction, Other users

Wet America – East: Irrigation for agriculture, Domestic and commercial, Manufacturing, Energy, Mineral extraction, Other users

How water in the west is used
(figures in billion litres)

660 – Irrigation for agriculture
345 – Domestic and commercial
205 – Manufacturing
105 – Energy
100 – Mineral extraction
120 – Other uses

ⓑ Use the evidence from your graph to give two ways in which the use of the water in the west of the USA differs from the use of water in the east of the USA.

Wet America

N ↑

CANADA

Mississippi R.

Ohio R.

Tennessee R.

GREAT LAKES CLEANUP
Before the 1972 Water Pollution Act, Lake Erie was a graveyard for fish. Now the lake is clean.

CLEVELAND
annual rainfall 889mm

WASHINGTON
annual rainfall 1064mm

ATLANTA
annual rainfall 1197mm

SHORTAGES AMID PLENTY
Even in the wet east, clean water can run short. Large populations, especially on the east coast, place severe strains on water supply facilities.

How water in the east is used
(figures in billion litres)

45 – Irrigation for agriculture
90 – Domestic and commercial
210 – Manufacturing
390 – Energy
20 – Minerals
5 – Other uses

775 billion litres of water per day withdrawn from resources.
12% not returned
88% used and returned

TENNESSEE VALLEY AUTHORITY
The nation's greatest river management system. The TVA brought shipping, flood control, recreation, hydro-electric power and jobs to a region with high unemployment.

0   200   400 km

SALTWATER
Taking large amounts of water from underground in Texas and Florida has led to saltwater from the sea seeping into wells.

ARKANSAS RIVER
This 650 kilometre canal has made an inland port of Tulsa in Oklahoma. It has also encouraged the growth of industry and provided recreation for the area.

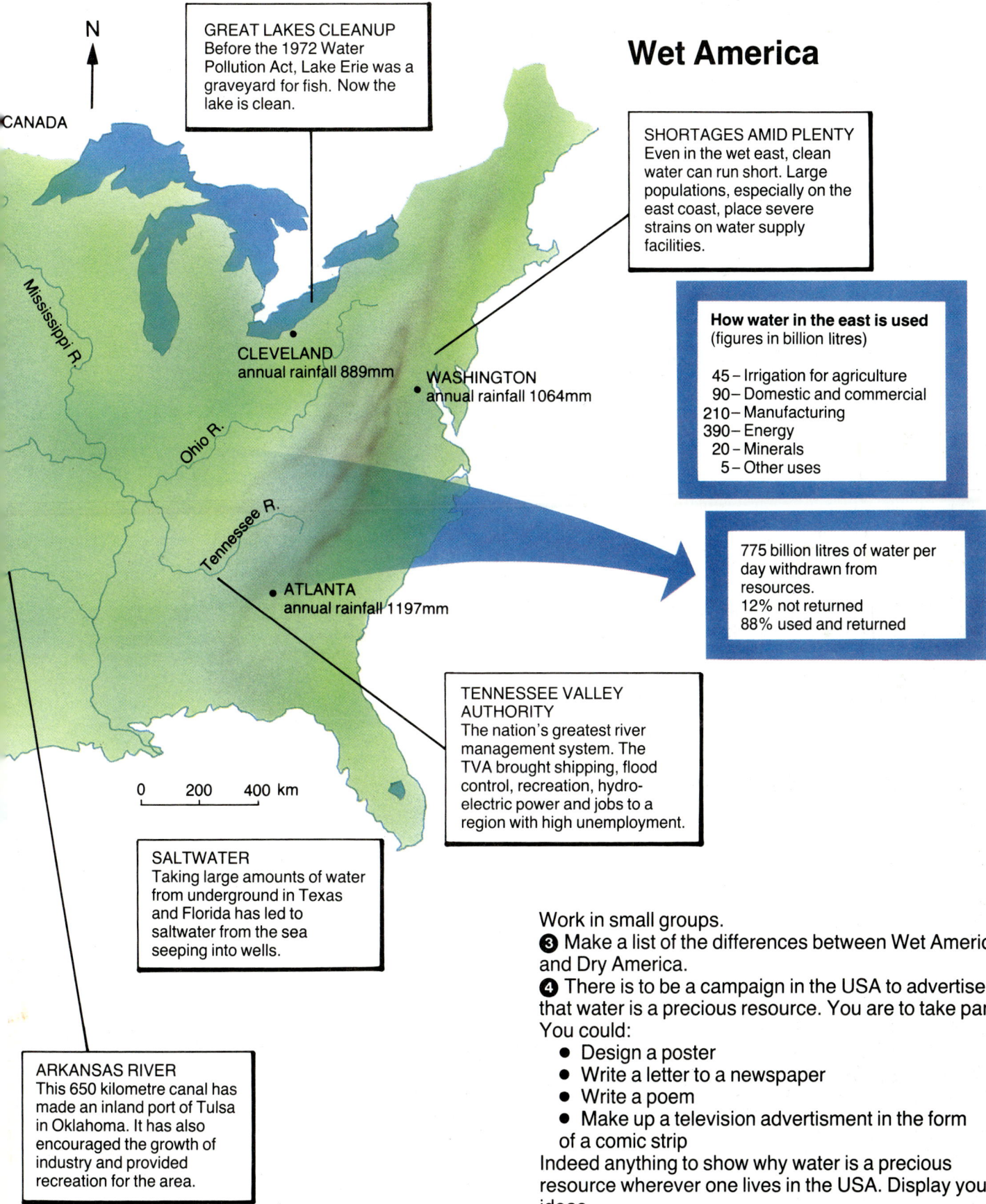

Work in small groups.
❸ Make a list of the differences between Wet America and Dry America.
❹ There is to be a campaign in the USA to advertise that water is a precious resource. You are to take part. You could:
   ● Design a poster
   ● Write a letter to a newspaper
   ● Write a poem
   ● Make up a television advertisment in the form of a comic strip
Indeed anything to show why water is a precious resource wherever one lives in the USA. Display your ideas.

9 SRI LANKA – ISLAND OF DREAMS?

Some countries were ruled by others in the past and they can still feel the effects. Why did Sri Lanka become a British colony? What problems does the country now face?

The pearl of the Indian Ocean is the way Sri Lanka is often described. With golden sands, a tropical climate and waving palms, it is a pearl indeed. You will receive a royal welcome from luxurious hotels and a people who will show you the delights of the island: the fabulous temples built ages ago in the depths of history; the beautiful scenery, green lush hills with luxurious vegetation.

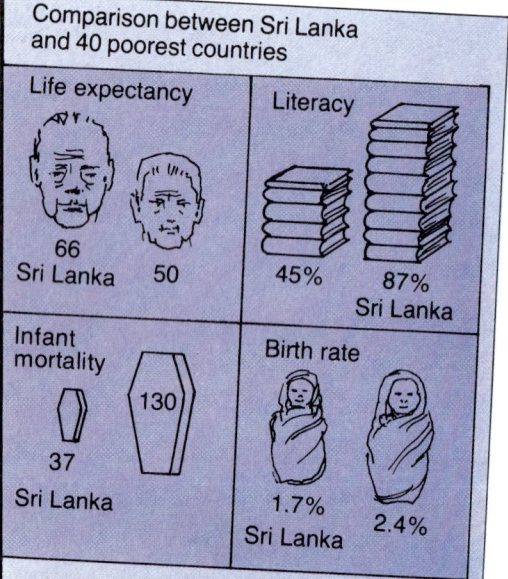

Comparison between Sri Lanka and 40 poorest countries

Life expectancy	Literacy
66 Sri Lanka 50	45% 87% Sri Lanka

Infant mortality	Birth rate
37 Sri Lanka 130	1.7% Sri Lanka 2.4%

Sri Lanka's population 15.3 million

PROGRESS

Year	Infant mortality rate (per 1000 live births)	Death rate (per 1000 of population)	Literacy rate
1946	141	19.8	57%
1950	82	12.6	—
1965	53	8.5	—
1977	42	6.4	—
1980	37	6.0	85%
1985	31	6.1	87%

❶ Enter this imaginary competition.
Win a holiday in Sri Lanka. All you have to do is:
ⓐ Write down four words which best describe the scene in the photographs of Sri Lanka.
ⓑ Complete the following sentence:
I would like to visit Sri Lanka because ....
....

❷ Write down three facts which the map in the brochure tells us about Sri Lanka.

❸ Look at the diagram above. Write out the following, using the correct word from each pair of brackets.
When we compare Sri Lanka with the other 40 poorest countries of the world we find that Sri Lanka has a (larger/smaller) percentage of people who can read; a (higher/lower) number of young children dying and people who can expect to live (shorter/longer) lives.

The coming of the British

For hundreds of years my people, the Kandyans, lived in the hills in the centre of what is now Sri Lanka. We were farmers growing our crops in clearings in the forest. The method of farming was called 'chena'. A patch of forest would be cut and burnt down and the crop planted. After a few years when the field became less fertile a new patch would be cleared. In this way the soil was kept fertile and was not washed away by the rain. As more people came to live here, these hillsides were TERRACED and used to grow rice.

A In 1795 our island was <u>invaded</u> by the British. They were traders, who by 1815, had <u>conquered</u> the whole of the island. When the British found that the Kandyan hills of Sri Lanka were ideal for growing coffee they began to <u>exploit</u> the area by <u>destroying</u> the forest and building roads into the hills. They renamed the country Ceylon.

B In 1840 the British passed a law giving much of our land to British landowners. They found that tea grew better than coffee in the hills, and <u>destroyed large areas of forest</u> to grow tea on large farms. This left us no land to farm in our traditional way and <u>we suffered greatly</u>.

C By 1890 tea had become the most important crop in Ceylon. Of course we Kandyans refused to work for the British invaders on their large farms. So the British forced many thousands of workers from Tamil Nadu in the south of India, which they also ruled, to work for them.

We did not drink tea, the plant did not grow in our country before the British came. They brought it from China. Most of the tea was sent to Britain for sale. The British had become great tea drinkers. The landowners and the tea companies became rich, we did not.

In 1948 British Rule ended. In 1972 Ceylon was officially renamed Sri Lanka.

4 ⓐ Write out paragraph **A** replacing the words underlined by the words below so that it seems as if it was written by a British author who believed the British presence in Ceylon was a good thing. Note that the words are in the wrong order:
clearing – visited – explored – develope
ⓑ Now write out either paragraph **B** or **C** and by changing a few words change the sense so that it seems as if it was written by the same British author.

The plantation

Picking tea

VISITOR: *Does all this land belong to the estate?*
ESTATE MANAGER: *Yes, all these bushes are ours.*
VISITOR: *What are these people doing?*
ESTATE MANAGER: *They are picking the small leaves at the end of the shoots on the tea bushes. They fill up the baskets which they carry on their backs.*
VISITOR: *What happens to the tea after it is picked?*
ESTATE MANAGER: *It is taken to the factory which you can see on the top of the hill and there it is left to ferment. Then it is dried and rolled.*
VISITOR: *Do you use machines for this?*
ESTATE MANAGER: *Yes, the tea bushes need a lot of people to care for them and pick the leaves but we use machines in the factory.*
VISITOR: *Is the tea then ready to send away?*
ESTATE MANAGER: *Yes. It is packed into large boxes called tea chests and sent to the port.*

❶ Match the labels in the list below with the correct letters from the photograph.
MANAGER'S HOUSE – WORKERS' HOUSES – FACTORY – WOODED HILLS – TEA PICKERS – NURSERY WHERE TEA BUSHES ARE GROWN BEFORE PLANTING ON HILLSIDE – ESTATE ROAD

❷ With the diagram below as a guide, use the words to draw a flow chart entitled 'Tea growing'.

DRYING – FERMENTING – PACKING – PICKING – ROLLING

❸ Suggest why there is a stick lying on the bushes in the foreground of the photograph.

> *I work as a tea picker on this estate. My name is Indrani. Each day I leave the house at about seven in the morning and spend about seven hours picking the small new shoots on the tea bushes. At the end of the day I will have picked about 27 kilograms of leaves which is about 10 thousand tips. This will make about 7 kilograms of tea to be sold. The leaves are weighed and I will be paid about 12 rupees for the day's work. In your money that is about 40 pence.*

Inside the workers' home. The whole family lives in this one room.

A 1980 UNICEF study found that conditions for estate workers were bad. Standards of housing, sewage disposal and water supply were poor. The proportion of housing under 25 square metres found in the estates was 64% compared with 28% in the villages and 27% in the towns and cities. It was not unusual for a family of five or six to be living, working, eating, sleeping and bringing up children in one small room, maybe with a front or back veranda.

Wages amongst the tea workers were below the average for Sri Lanka. Death rates were high and many people suffered from MALNUTRITION.

❹ Work in pairs: Imagine that you are government officials in Sri Lanka. You have a small amount of money to make two changes which will help the workers on a tea estate in the Kandy district. Decide which two of the following five changes would be of the greatest benefit to the estate workers:

    ⓐ adding a room to each worker's living quarters
    ⓑ building a sewage system
    ⓒ providing a clinic
    ⓓ constructing a cinema
    ⓔ establishing a school for the estate worker's children.

❺ ⓐ *In what ways are the descriptions of the estates given on these two pages different?*
  ⓑ *Suggest reasons for the different descriptions.*

The tea trade

The tea producing countries – (numbers) indicate thousands of tonnes

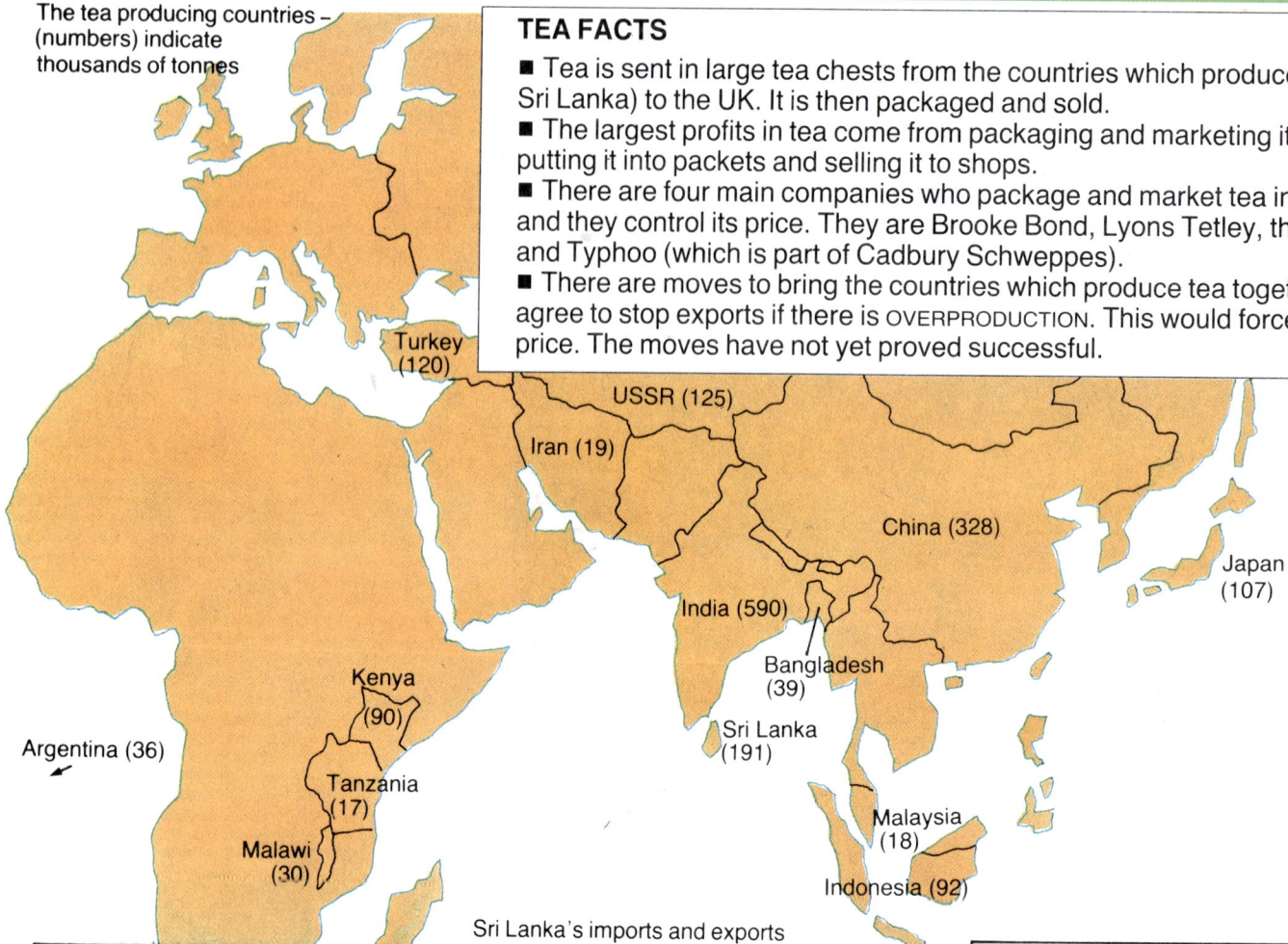

Turkey (120)

USSR (125)

Iran (19)

China (328)

Japan (107)

India (590)

Bangladesh (39)

Kenya (90)

Sri Lanka (191)

Argentina (36)

Tanzania (17)

Malaysia (18)

Malawi (30)

Indonesia (92)

Sri Lanka's imports and exports

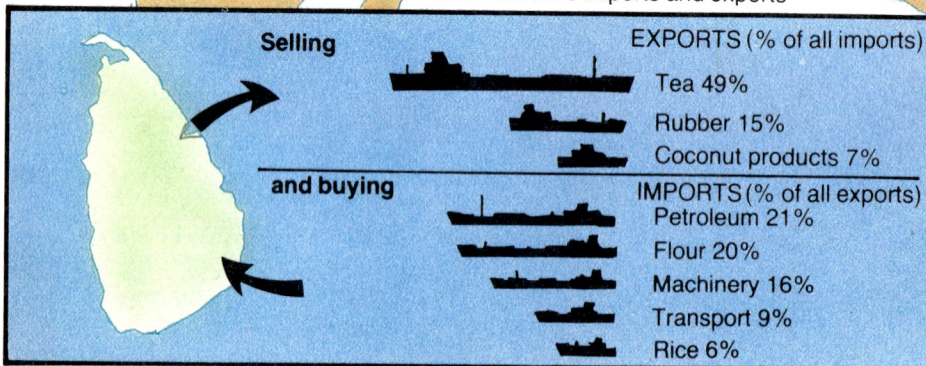

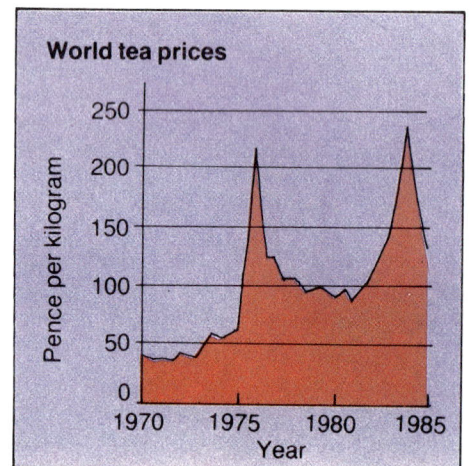

Selling

EXPORTS (% of all imports)

Tea 49%

Rubber 15%

Coconut products 7%

and buying

IMPORTS (% of all exports)

Petroleum 21%

Flour 20%

Machinery 16%

Transport 9%

Rice 6%

World tea prices

Pence per kilogram

250 200 150 100 50 0

1970 1975 1980 1985

Year

❶ From the map above make a list of the tea producing countries in order, from the largest producer to the smallest producer (in rank order).

❷ Use the map above and an atlas to describe the route the ships carrying the tea are likely to take from Sri Lanka to the UK.

❸ Why does the fact that there are only four main companies buying and selling tea in the UK help them to keep the price of tea low?

❹ Look at the diagram of 'Selling and buying' on the left. Why are tea prices so important for Sri Lanka?

❺ Look at the graph of world tea prices above. What has happened to the price of tea since 1970?

❻ *Why would the price of tea be forced up if the producing countries all agreed to withhold exports?*

A multinational changes?

Brooke Bond is a MULTINATIONAL company. It has offices and owns companies in many countries. Like all multinationals, it is large and owns companies which control all the various stages of the tea business. Its companies obtain the tea, and they also organise its transport and sale.

Some people in Britain, who were angry at the low prices Sri Lanka was receiving for tea and the conditions on the estates, bought shares in Brooke Bond and protested at the annual shareholders' meeting. Others who felt the same way have protested outside supermarkets.

SRI LANKA NATIONALISES THE PLANTATIONS

With the land reforms of 1972 and 1975, Sri Lanka took over units of tea growing land of over 50 acres which were owned by private individuals or companies. More than 60% of all tea lands and all the larger estates are now state-owned.

During the first ten years of NATIONALISATION the amount of tea produced has dropped. Bad management, the sending back of many skilled Tamil workers to India, as well as arguments amongst the workers, have all helped to cause the drop in tea output.

The rich countries still have control of the price of tea because they control its transport, packaging and marketing. Many of those who have replaced the Indian Tamil workers on the estates do not have the same skill and experience in tea growing. Quality has dropped. Costs of fertilisers and other imports have risen.

However, the government is offering money to encourage 130 000 farmers to plant tea on small plots. This, and a steady improvement in the running of the estates, is gradually improving the quality and output. Conditions for the workers on the estates are improving only very slowly.

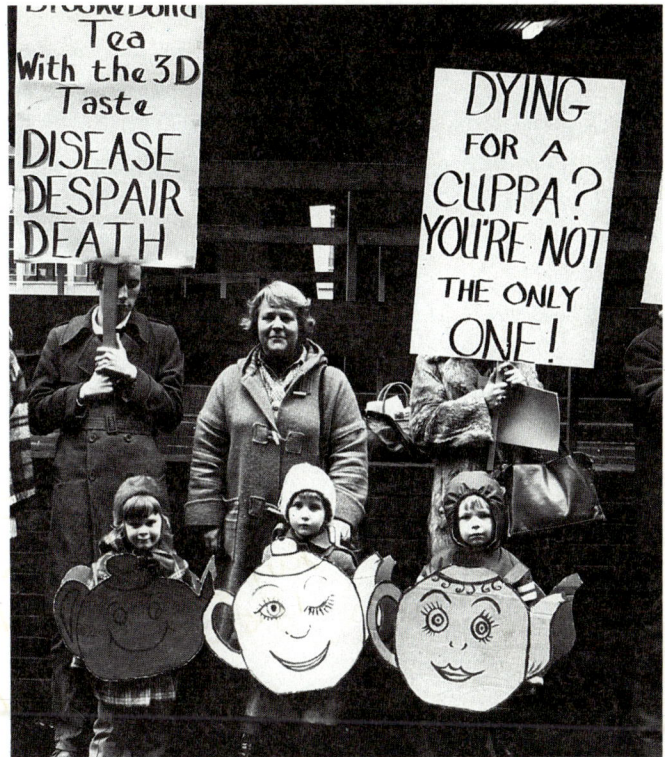

Protesters outside a supermarket

2 APRIL 1999

THE GAZETTE

COST OF TEA DOUBLES OVERNIGHT

Tomorrow the packet of tea you buy in your local supermarket will cost twice what it does today.

There is expected to be a rush to buy the last remaining stocks of cheap tea. Companies have been forced to raise their prices as tea producing countries across the world have pushed up the price of tea.

7 ⓐ Imagine that you took part in the protest shown in the photograph. Give one reason why you might have joined this protest.

ⓑ Join with a neighbour and read the information on nationalisation on the left. Imagine that you are the press officers of the company against whom the demonstration above is being held. Write down your reply to a newspaper reporter who asks you for a statement about the protest.

8 How do you think tea drinkers in the UK would react if the price of tea doubled overnight? Could they do anything about it? Discuss your answers with your neighbour.

The Tamils and the Sinhalese

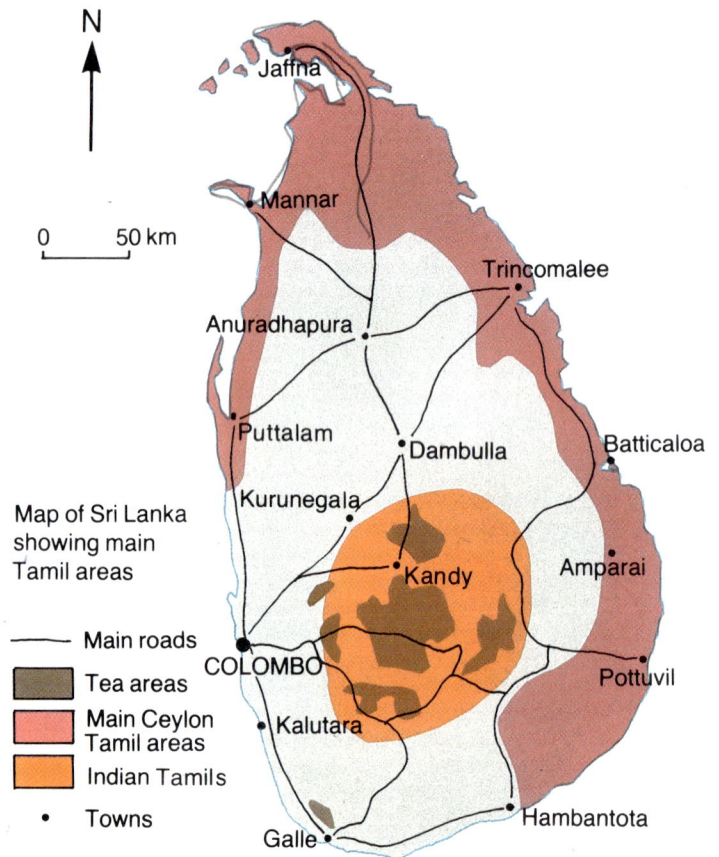

Map of Sri Lanka showing main Tamil areas

- Main roads
- Tea areas
- Main Ceylon Tamil areas
- Indian Tamils
- Towns

The Sinhalese people are BUDDHIST. They make up the largest group of people on the island and have lived there for centuries.

There are two distinct Tamil communities in Sri Lanka. All are HINDUS. One group known as the Ceylon Tamils have lived on the island for hundreds of years. The other group are the Indian Tamils who were brought from southern India during the nineteenth century to work on tea plantations.

Many of the Indian Tamils have moved to the north of the island to join the Ceylon Tamil communities. This is because trouble has arisen between the Tamils and the Sinhalese.

❶ Use the map of Sri Lanka above to describe the main areas where:
ⓐ Ceylon Tamils live;
ⓑ Indian Tamils live.

❷ Look at the information on this page and think about the rest of this chapter. Suggest three reasons why there is unrest between the Tamils and the Sinhalese.

TWO KINGDOMS

When the first European invaders, the Portuguese, arrived in the 16th century, they found quite separate ancient kingdoms in Sri Lanka: Tamils in the north and Sinhalese in the south. The kingdoms remained separate under the Portuguese and the Dutch who came later. It was not until the arrival of the British in the 19th century that they were brought under one rule.

Ten Tamils killed in backlash to massacre

Sri Lanka numbed by terrorist slaughter

Tamil workers massacred in paddy fields

HOSTILITY

Hostility between the Tamils and the Sinhalese has pushed Sri Lanka to the brink of civil war. The Sinhalese are the majority, but 2.5 million Tamils live in Sri Lanka, and over half of these have lived on the island for as long as the Sinhalese. Matters got worse in the 1960s and 1970s when the government saw that it could become very popular by favouring the Sinhalese rather than the Tamils.

Sinhalese, rather than Tamil, has become the official language. Tamils receive poorer schooling and find it difficult to get jobs in government services. A new scheme was introduced to send 600,000 Tamils back to India, even though they had been in Sri Lanka for over a hundred years. Tamil plantation workers had their Sri Lankan citizenship removed. As a result of this some Tamils began to demand a separate Tamil state. The next step was that the Tamil political party was banned from government.

Fighting broke out and continues today. One of the Tamil armed organisations is known as the Tigers. Many Tamils have fled to Jaffna, in the north of the country, and many other educated Tamils have left the country for good. Their skills have been lost to Sri Lanka.

For the time being, an uneasy peace has been restored to the country through an agreement between the Indian government and the Sri Lankan government. Indian soldiers are stationed in the North. Most of the Tigers have given up their weapons.

But, if future trouble is to be avoided the government must still tackle poverty and DISCRIMINATION.

❸ Imagine that you are a Tamil worker on a tea estate who was offered a small sum of money and a ticket to go to India. Your neighbour too is offered REPATRIATION. Discuss how you would feel, and decide what you would do.

❹ Imagine that you are Sinhalese and that a member of your family has been killed on the train shown above. Describe how you would feel towards the Tamils who blew up the train.

Why not investigate?

Research into a crop which is grown outside Europe such as coffee, sugar or bananas. You could find out:
- where it is grown;
- how it is grown;
- what it is like to be a worker on a farm or plantation;
- how the crop is brought to the UK and sold.

You could display your work.

10 PEOPLE AND SPACE

In South Africa RACIST laws have been passed to create the apartheid system under which people are not free to live or work where they choose. The apartheid system gives parts of the country to different races. Why and how has this system developed?

Apartheid

Apartheid means the system by which the white South African government separates groups of people according to their race. Black people have no vote and are not allowed to play a part in the government of their country. Almost everyone in the world agrees that the apartheid system is racist and wrong.

The South African government divides people into four racial groups:

BLACKS – the African negro population.
WHITES – mostly people of British or Dutch descent. Those of Dutch descent, the Afrikaners, make up 60% of the white population.
COLOUREDS – people of mixed race.
ASIANS – are descended mainly from Indians, Chinese and Malays.
Note: All non-white groups consider themselves 'Black'. For simplicity, during this unit, we will refer to groups of people by the terms above.

Population by race groups in South Africa

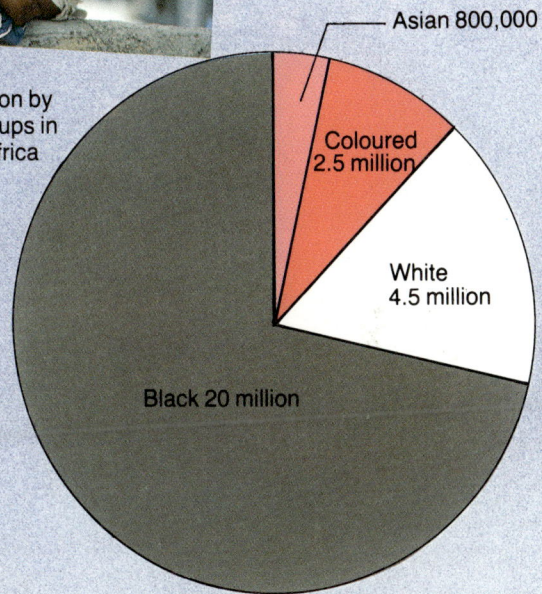

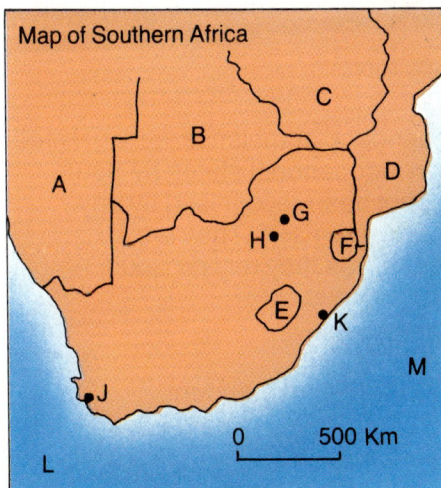

- Asian 800,000
- Coloured 2.5 million
- White 4.5 million
- Black 20 million

Map of Southern Africa

0   500 Km

❶ Look at the map of southern Africa on the left. Use your atlas to name:
ⓐ the countries A, B, C, D, E and F;
ⓑ the towns G, H, J and K;
ⓒ the seas L and M.

❷ In South Africa the apartheid system gives parts of the country to different races so that the Whites have 87% of the land and the Blacks only 13%.
ⓐ Draw a pie chart to show the division of land in South Africa.
Compare your chart with the one above. What does this tell us about land ownership under apartheid?

❸ Draw a framework for a graph like the one shown below. Using the figures given next to the framework and those in the pie chart above:
ⓐ Draw a line graph on the framework showing the population change for Black people. Label the line. Do the same for Whites, Coloureds and Asians.
ⓑ Continue the lines up to the year 2000.
ⓒ If present trends continue what will the population of each group be in the year 2000?

❹ Look at the photographs opposite. What do they tell us about South Africa?

❺ Join with a neighbour and look at the photograph on this page. Discuss and write down how this illustrates apartheid. Why do people see this as racist and wrong?

Growth of population of South Africa (millions)

	1960	1970	1980
Blacks	11	15	20
Whites	3	3.75	4.5
Coloured	1.5	2	2.5
Asian	0.5	0.6	0.8

Population of South Africa

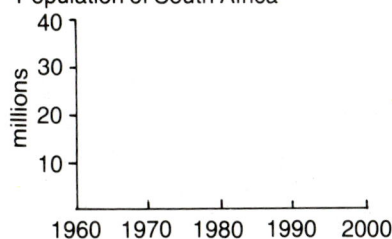

millions
40
30
20
10

1960 1970 1980 1990 2000

Living apart – Homelands

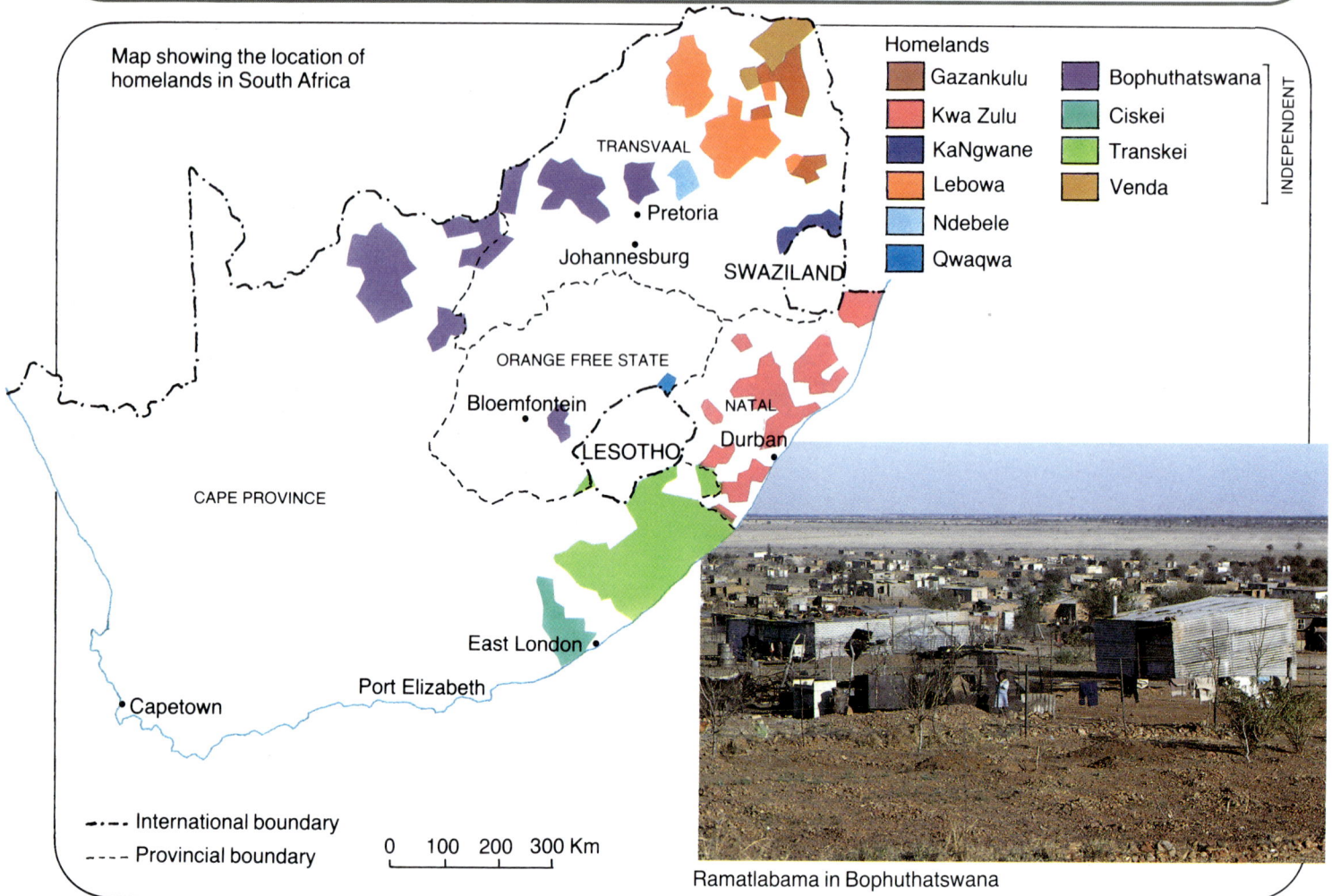

Map showing the location of homelands in South Africa

Homelands

Gazankulu		Bophuthatswana	
Kwa Zulu		Ciskei	
KaNgwane		Transkei	
Lebowa		Venda	
Ndebele			
Qwaqwa			

INDEPENDENT

TRANSVAAL

• Pretoria

Johannesburg

SWAZILAND

ORANGE FREE STATE

Bloemfontein •

NATAL

Durban

LESOTHO

CAPE PROVINCE

East London •

Port Elizabeth

• Capetown

-·-·- International boundary
- - - - Provincial boundary

0   100   200   300 Km

Ramatlabama in Bophuthatswana

The 1959 Promotion of Bantu Self-Government Act was the start of the homelands or 'Bantustans'. All Blacks were to be members of a 'homeland' which would be the only place where they would have the right to vote, despite the fact that they may never have seen or had any connection with the area. The first 'Bantustan', Transkei, received some self-government in 1963.

Blacks make up over 70% of the population and yet the homelands cover only 13% of the country. They are also on the poorest land in the country and extremely hard to farm. Hundreds of thousands of black people have been uprooted from their houses and forced to move to these areas.

Blacks are sent to a homeland where their language is spoken. Many Blacks feel this is a senseless division. The homelands simply divide people and provide a supply of labour for the mines and institutions owned by the Whites. Only Blacks employed in South Africa are allowed to go to South Africa. Their families may not go with them and they have to remain in their homeland. The 'independent' homelands were granted the status of sovereign independent states by South Africa, this status has not been recognised by any other country or the UNITED NATIONS. They are independent in name only, as they rely on South Africa for all their needs.

❶ Using the map above:
ⓐ Which is the largest of the independent homelands?
ⓑ Why is this difficult to answer?

❷ ⓐ Measure how far it is for someone in Transkei to travel to work in Johannesburg.
ⓑ What will this mean for the family if only the worker can go?

❸ Look at the photograph of the homeland of Bophuthatswana. Imagine you have been brought here by the South African Authorities. What would your feelings be on seeing it for the first time?

❹ Lesotho and Swaziland are not homelands. Find out what their status is from books in the library.

Living apart – Townships

One aspect of apartheid is shown by the map of Johannesburg below. The Group Areas Act of 1950 allowed the government to decide where people were to live. People 'entitled' to live in towns and cities were divided, by their race, into separate residential areas. In the case of Blacks these were the townships. These were built well away from the town itself, with poor housing and AMENITIES and with limited transport to the places of work. Blacks were resettled in the new townships.

The largest of the townships is Soweto. Soweto has a population of well over one million. After riots in 1976 the government started some programmes to improve conditions but FACILITIES are still very poor.

Soweto Township, Johannesburg

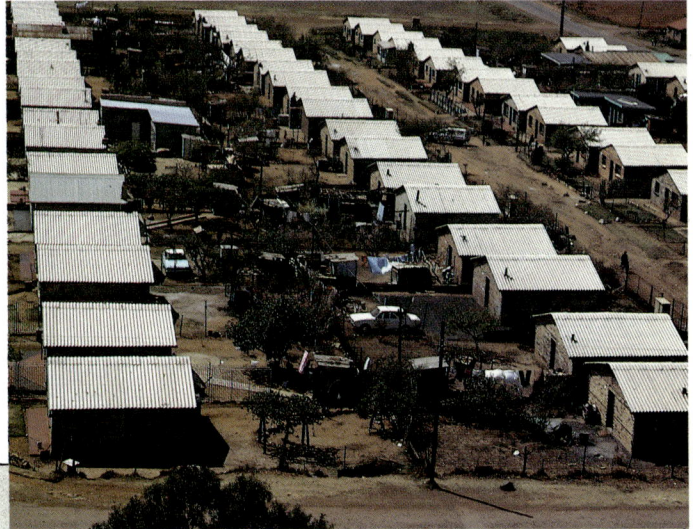

The Townships of Johannesburg

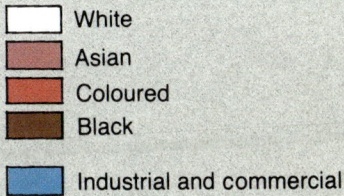

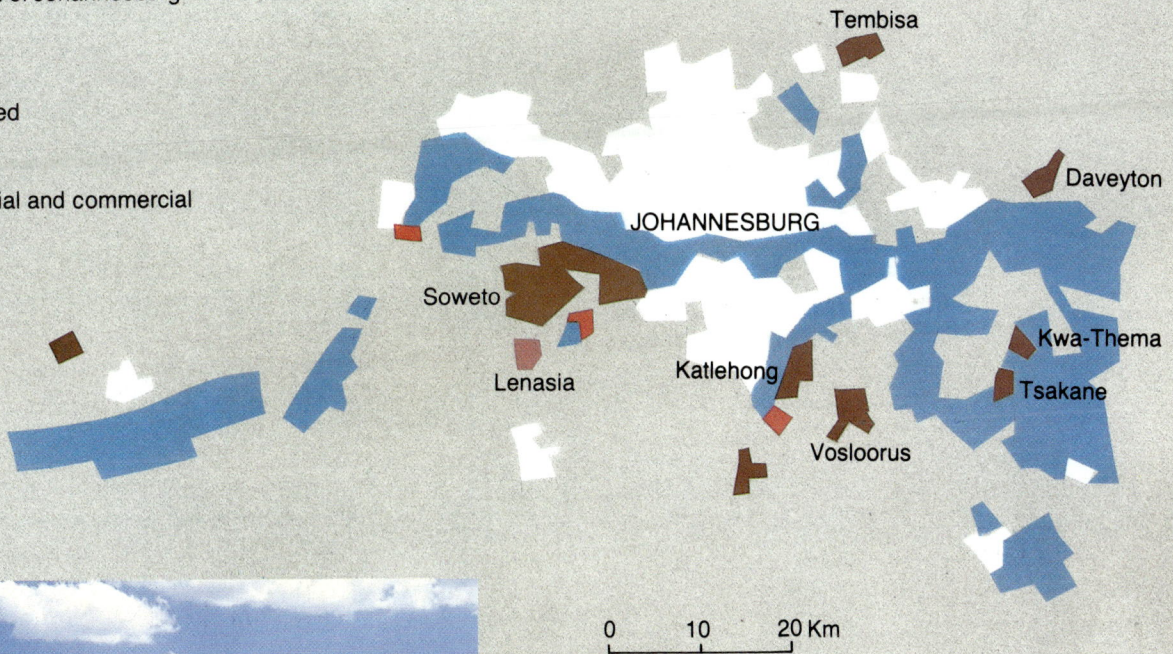

- White
- Asian
- Coloured
- Black
- Industrial and commercial

Tembisa
Daveyton
JOHANNESBURG
Soweto
Kwa-Thema
Lenasia
Katlehong
Tsakane
Vosloorus

0   10   20 Km

White residential area, Johannesburg

5 Using the map of Johannesburg above:
ⓐ Measure the distance from east to west and from north to south across Soweto.
ⓑ What separates Soweto from the white areas of Johannesburg?
ⓒ Why do you think the Blacks were not moved even further from the city?

6 Look at the photographs of Soweto and the white residential area of Johannesburg. What do they tell us about who benefited from the Group Areas Act?

People and settlement – conflict for land

1 The area we now know as South Africa has been lived in for thousands of years. The San peoples whose descendents still live there today, lived by hunting game and gathering fruit and vegetation. Many of their beautiful rock paintings still survive. The Khoikoi people herded flocks of sheep. About 1 500 years ago people who spoke Bantu languages, such as the Xhosa, the Zulus and Tswanas, began to move southwards.

Towards the end of the nineteenth century the Zulus became the strongest group in eastern South Africa and expanded their lands very rapidly.

Rock paintings like this were painted by the San people for many thousands of years before the Europeans arrived. They were an important part of San culture.

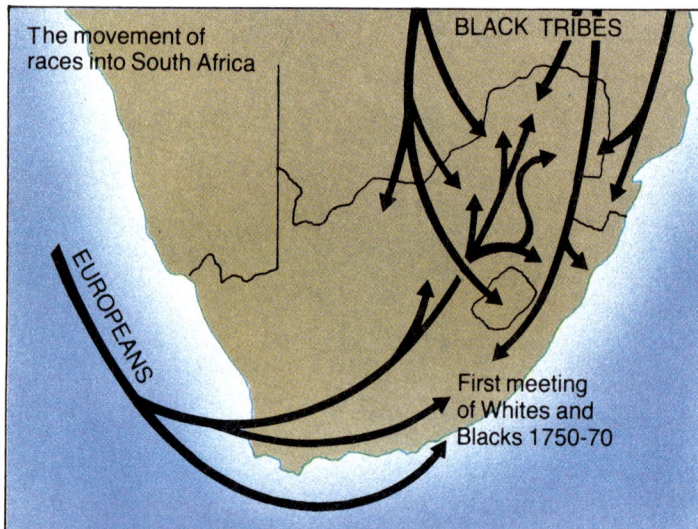

The movement of races into South Africa

BLACK TRIBES

EUROPEANS

First meeting of Whites and Blacks 1750-70

2 Meanwhile, in 1652, the Dutch led by Jan van Riebeck established a small settlement of about 90 people at the Cape of Good Hope. As their numbers grew they took away the land of the San and Khoi peoples by force. The Dutch became known as Boers or farmers.

The British arrived in 1806. They declared the Cape a British colony. Land became scarce. The Boers had many African slaves who worked the land, but as land became harder to get they began to move further into the country. In 1833 the British introduced anti-slavery laws and the Boers were horrified. The British replaced the anti-slavery laws with severe master/servant laws where Black people were often jailed for minor offences.

3 The need for more land and the wish to move away from British control made the Boers leave the Cape. Between 1836 and 1846 about 14 000 Boers left the colony with their sheep, cattle, ox carts and servants. This was the Great Trek. After driving the Bantu peoples, particularly the Zulus with the help of the British, from the land, they settled in Orange Free State and Transvaal.

Then diamonds were found in Kimberley and gold in the Transvaal. The British decided to annex the Transvaal in 1877 and when the Boers realised they would take the Orange Free State as well, they declared war in 1899. Three years later the Boers surrendered and in 1910 the Union of South Africa including all of South Africa was established as a self-governing dominion within the British Empire.

The Great Trek

... and resources

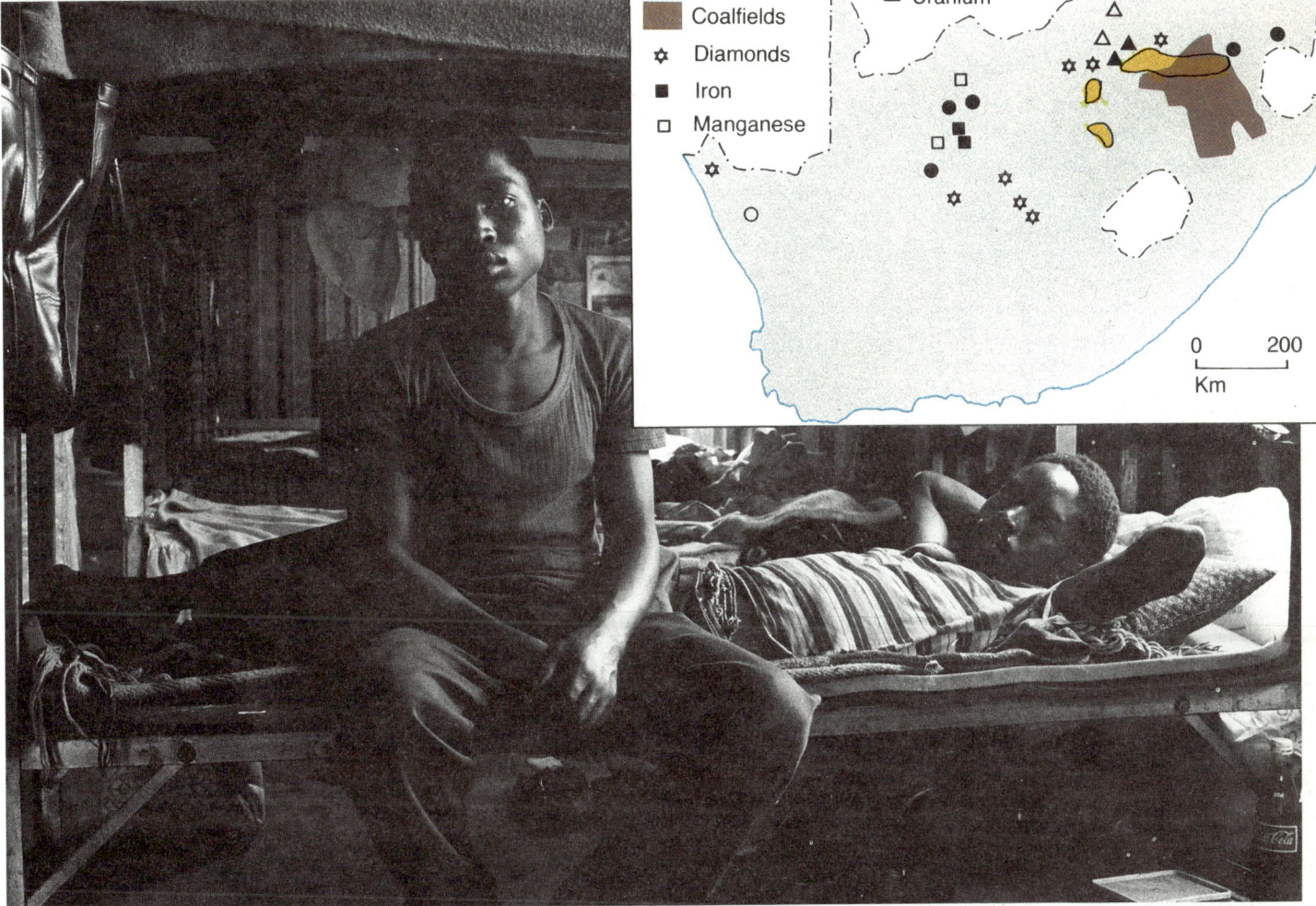

The mineral resources of South Africa

○ Copper
● Asbestos
△ Platinum
▲ Uranium

Goldfields
Coalfields
✪ Diamonds
■ Iron
□ Manganese

0   200
Km

Men's hostel for migrant workers in Alexandra, Johannesburg

The Black people of South Africa are the workers in the mines and factories. Many of the workers are MIGRANTS. They live in a compound or dormitory at the place where they work and only go home to their family at the end of their contract, which usually lasts a year. Over one-third of these migrants now come from the homelands, a decreasing number come from neighbouring countries. This means that the women are left to look after the land, home and children for much of the time. If work is scarce then South Africa does not need the workers and they are sent home. South Africa refuses to care for the unemployed as they come from other countries or the homelands. The people are a 'reservoir' of labour for South Africa.

Other Black workers are commuters, living in the townships several miles outside the cities and travelling to work. Every day about 250 000 people travel from Soweto on 100 trains to work in Johannesburg. Some travel daily from the homelands to nearby industrial areas.

❶ What does the picture of the San rock paintings tell us about the people who made things like this?

❷ Imagine that you were an African seeing the Boers passing on the Great Trek. Write down what you would have seen and your feelings about seeing them crossing into your land.

❸ Using the key to the map of mineral resources above:
ⓐ Make a list of the main minerals mined in South Africa.
ⓑ Describe where most minerals in South Africa are found.
ⓒ Look back to the map of the homelands on page 76. Which homelands are best placed for workers to travel regularly to the mines?

❹ ⓐ What is the difference between workers who are 'migrants' and those who are 'commuters'?
ⓑ Which system has the most effect on family life?

❺ *In pairs, decide what is meant by the description of the homelands as a 'reservoir of labour' for South Africa.*

Apartheid

Reality

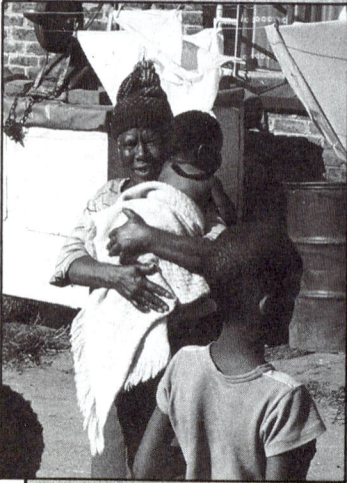

One day the police came and moved us to this place in Bophuthatswana. We used to have a little land to grow food. Here there is not enough land to grow anything, and no work. We didn't want to come. My son had to go to work in the mines near Johannesburg, he doesn't like the work, it is very dangerous. He lives in a hostel with hundreds of others, he gets paid very little and sends as much as he can to me. His wife, whom he rarely sees, works as a domestic worker for a white family. I am looking after their three children as best I can but we have nothing. The children don't know their mother or father, we see their mother once a month on her day off and their father for one month a year when he is allowed home. There is no life here for us, no hope, there is nothing, it gets no better.

WELFARE

Infant deaths per 1000 live births

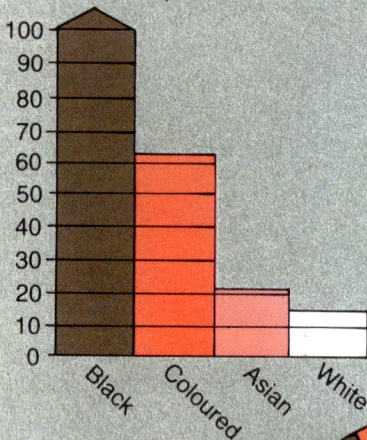

Tuberculosis cases per 100 000 people

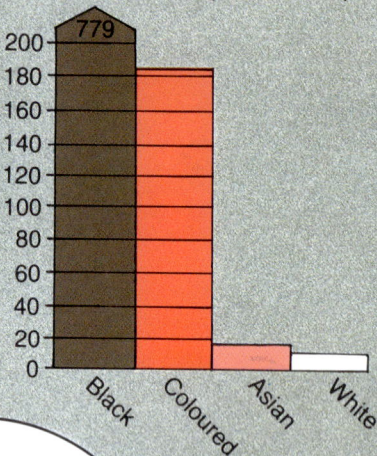

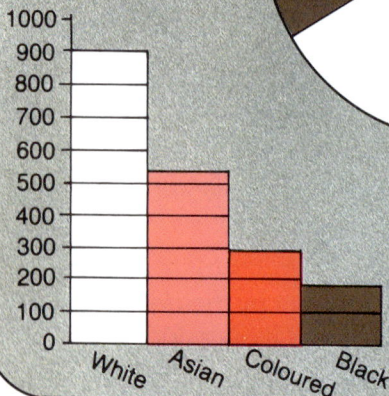
Income by race group in South Africa

Amount spent on each school pupil (rand)

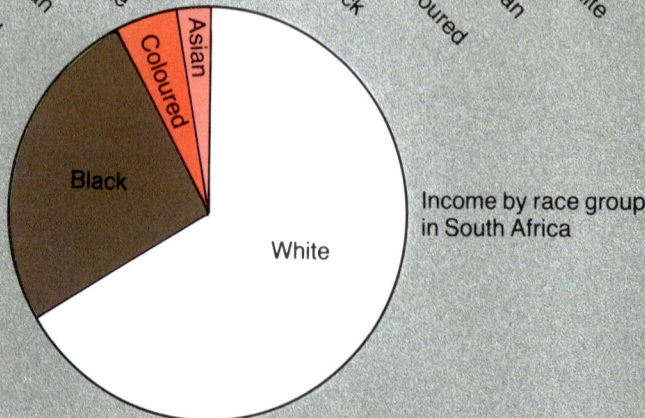

Number of pupils per teacher

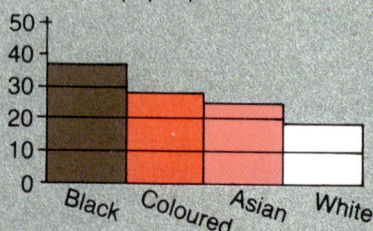

Dreaming of a better world

❶ Make two columns like those below and fill in the gaps using the information on welfare.

South Africa – Equality?

Whites 4.5 million		Blacks 20 million
64%	Income	26%
	Infant deaths per 1000	
	No. of pupils per teacher	39
	Amount spent on each school pupil	
10	TB case per 100,000	

❷ What does your chart tell you about the inequality of apartheid?

❸ Imagine that you are one of the children living with your grandmother in Bophuthatswana. Write down what you might tell someone who asked about your life. (Use information from the tables and the information elsewhere in the unit to help.)

❹ What is the dream of the future which is illustrated in the poem by Richard Rive?

Protest – will there be change?

Black people in South Africa have protested against apartheid for many years. They have been joined in this protest by Coloured and Asian people and some Whites.

THE PEOPLE OF SOUTH AFRICA HAVE URGED THEIR FRIENDS OVERSEAS TO ISOLATE SOUTH AFRICA. YOU CAN BEGIN NOW –

Boycott South African Goods

These labels are often to be found on packages containing South African goods.

(By law the country of origin must be on the package)

Watch the label and boycott these:

Canned Meats	Canned Fruit	Express	Fresh Fruit
Apex	Gold Reef	Cokiale	Cape
Armour Star	IXL	Planter's Pride	Golden Jubilee
Honeycure	Koo		Outspan
Double Crown	RFF	**Wines**	Impl
Maconochie	Summerlow	S A Hock	(Apples, grapes,
Union	Southern Pride	S A Burgundy	oranges, etc.)
Prime	Summit (Bartlett)	Richelieu	
	Spa	Van der Hum	**Cheese**
Canned Fish	Topflite	Oudameestar	Farmer's Union
Cape Pride	Hamlet	Chateau Libering	
Corsair	Dwyars River	Grumbergan Stein	**Pet Food**
Glenrych	Hugo	La Gratitude	Happy Pet Cat Food
Winrey	Avalon	JUR Liqueur	
Armour	Silver Leaf	Rembrandt	
John West	Libby's	La Residence	
Puffin	Planter's		

– and all other South African products. Fourteen per cent of South Africa's exports to Britain are foodstuffs.

5 ⓐ Look at the list of South African goods. List *three* of the names you have seen in your local supermarket.

ⓑ The advertisement is suggesting that we should help the Black people in South Africa. How does it suggest we do this?

ⓒ Would you be prepared to boycott South African goods or not? Give your reasons. You might want to think about the effects boycotts may have on Black workers in South Africa.

6 Look at the quotations on the right, from the official South African publications.

ⓐ Which group is missing from the parliament? Look back through this unit. Are they a large group?

A new constitution?

'... in November 1983 the White electorate approved by a large majority a new constitution which will grant the Coloured and Indian communities autonomy in their own affairs and co-responsibility with Whites for all matters of national importance. When the new system is implemented, Coloureds and Indians will have their own Houses in the Central Parliament on the same basis as Whites.'

From *This is South Africa* compiled by the publications division of the Department of Foreign Affairs – Pretoria, March 1984

South Africa's new constitution was implemented in September 1984. The Parliament consists of three Houses:

The House of Assembly – 178 members – directly elected by Whites.

The House of Representatives – 85 members – directly elected by Coloureds.

The House of Delegates – 45 members – directly elected by Indians.

'Because provision has been made through the political and economic development of the Black national states to satisfy the needs and aspirations of the Black peoples, the government has rejected all representations that the Blacks shoud be represented on the President's Council and in Parliament.'

From *Official Yearbook of the Republic of South Africa 1985.*

ⓑ What are the 'Black national states'?

ⓒ Imagine you are a Black South African. Write a paragraph giving your point of view about these statements.

Why not investigate?

Make a poster of any recent newspaper cuttings on South Africa. List any new developments in the country, and discuss them with others.

11 FEEDING A BILLION PEOPLE

China has 25% of the world's population but only 7% of the world's populated land. To feed all its people is a major challenge. The Chinese have lived under political systems which have attempted to meet this challenge in different ways.

Information about the four most populated countries in the world

Country	Area ('000 km^2)	Population (millions)	Density of population per km^2
China	9 600	1 035	108
India	3 300	746	198
USA	9 400	236	25
USSR	22 400	274	12

China's land use (%)	
Arable	11
Pasture	31
Woodland	13
Rest	45

❶ Study the four photographs above the tables.
ⓐ Write a paragraph to describe the scene shown in each photograph.
ⓑ For each photograph decide whether you think the land could be used to provide food for China's people. Explain your answer.

❷ Look carefully at the table on the left and then copy and complete the following sentences:
ⓐ The country with the biggest population is ____ .
ⓑ The largest country is _____ .
ⓒ The country with the greatest density of population is _____ .

❸ Use the figures from 'China's land use' to draw a divided bar graph. Label it clearly.

❹ Name two sorts of land which might be included under the heading 'Rest'.

The land of China

Beijing

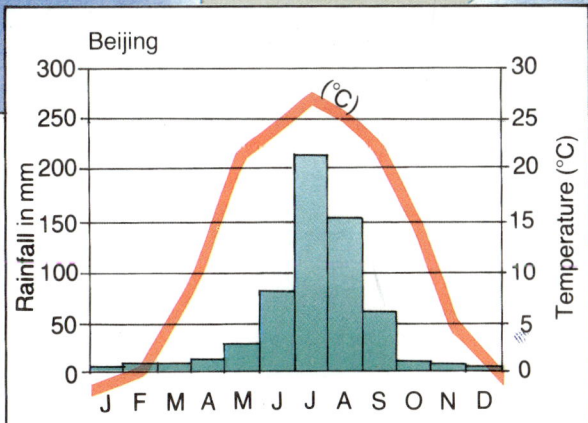

Guangzhou

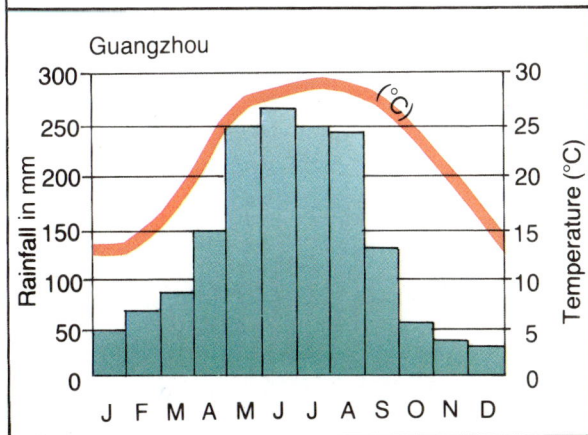

❺ Look at the map above.
ⓐ What is the distance in kilometres from:
   (i) Beijing to Guangzhou?
   (ii) Shanghai to Chongqing?
ⓑ What is the direction from:
   (i) Chongqing to Shenyang?
   (ii) Tianjin to Nanjing?
ⓒ Write a sentence to state:
   (i) How many cities there are in China with a population of over 1 million.
   (ii) In which part of the country those cities are found.

❻ Name five countries which share a border with China.

❼ Draw two columns in your book, one headed Beijing, the other Guangzhou. Write each statement below in one column or both columns to describe the climates shown in the graphs on the left.

■ More rainfall in summer.   ■ Warm winter.
■ Frost in winter.   ■ Heavier rain.
■ Winter is almost dry.   ■ Hot summer.

Before 1949 ...

The pattern of life in the Chinese countryside has not changed for hundreds of years. There were landlords, some very rich, and peasants, mostly very poor. Su Ling is now an old man. He remembers the way he and his father farmed land near Wuhan, on the Chang Jiang River, in the years before 1949.

Su Ling

My father had a farm of one hectare*. It was divided into small plots, some on good land, some on bad. They were far apart, so a lot of time was wasted carrying seeds or seedlings, or a plough, from one plot to another.

We paid 50% of the crop to our landlord as rent. We were often in debt to the landlord or to the merchants. They controlled our lives. It was hard work but still we did not have enough to eat.

Rice was the main crop. We sowed it in a seed bed in April. The seedlings were transplanted in May when they were 20 cm high. The rice grew in water which had to be raised from canals with a hand pump.

In August the fields were drained and the harvest began. Everything was done by hand. When they were clear the fields were sown in September with wheat or beans. They grew in the winter and were harvested in April.

We also grew some vegetables like cabbages or sweet corn. Sometimes we grew melons, a great luxury. We never had meat but we occasionally caught fish in the ponds or canals.

The rain was very unreliable. Some years there was little and the rice crop failed. Other years there was too much and the crop was destroyed. We could not control the water.

* 1 hectare is about the size of two football pitches.

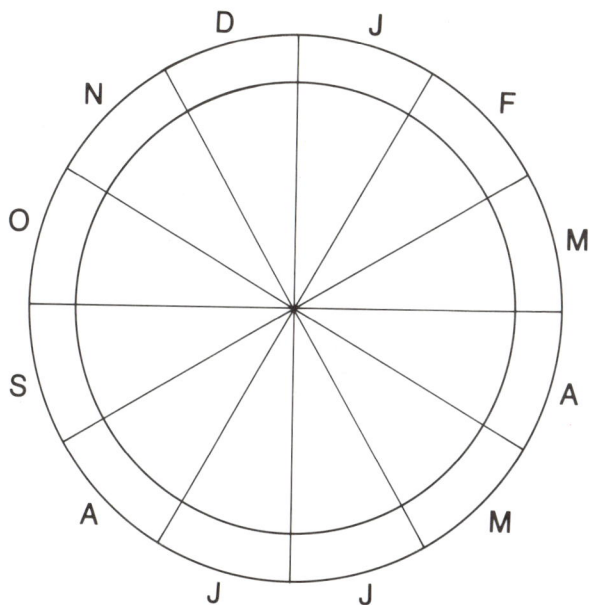

The circular diagram shows the months around a circle: D, J, F, M, A, M, J, J, A, S, O, N.

1   Draw a large circular diagram like the one above to record the growing cycle which Su Ling describes on the previous page.

ⓐ In the outer circle shade blue the months April to August to show they are the wettest months in Wuhan.

ⓑ Shade in another colour, the months when rice is being grown. Write Sowing, Transplanting and Harvest in the correct months.

ⓒ Shade in another colour the months when wheat and beans are being grown. Write Sowing and Harvest in the correct months.

ⓓ Add a key.

2 How do you think the crops grown relate to the weather conditions?

3 It is said the Chinese farmers in this part of the country 'make one hectare become two hectares'. What do you think this means?

4 State three ways in which the life of Su Ling and his family was very hard.

5 How do you think the landlord and merchant controlled his life?

6 Study the photograph below.
ⓐ Briefly describe what the photograph shows.
ⓑ Why do you think a truck could not be used to carry seedlings or implements?
ⓒ Why are the mud banks necessary?

7 State one advantage and one disadvantage about widely scattered plots.

Sichuan Province, China

Changes in the countryside after 1949

The Communist Revolution led by Mao Zedong overthrew the landlords and tried to rule China for the benefit of all its people.

Mao Zedong

Commune workers holding a meeting

How the changes came about

1949–52 Land taken from landlords and rich peasants and shared out between all who worked on the land.

1952–54 Mutual Aid Teams were formed. Land was still privately owned but groups of about ten families were encouraged to work together. They could work for each other and make full use of their implements and work animals.

1955–58 Co-operatives were formed. All land was pooled together and worked by 200–300 households. The crops were shared between the people who grew them.

1959–79 Communes were made by joining many co-operatives together. A commune might have 40 000 people. It would be responsible for water control, forestry, education and health as well as farming. All families had a basic food ration.

Su Ling's son, Su Yun, explains how the commune is organised.

We each work in a **production team** of about 20 families. We work a piece of land and look after the machinery and animals. About 15 production teams make a **brigade** which is similar to a village. **The brigade** looks after its water supply, repairs farm machinery and processes the farm crops.

As many as 20 brigades form a **commune**. The commune can organise factories, reclaim land, plant trees, build dams or roads. The decisions are made by a committee which represents all the people. We can have much greater control over our life now.

❷ Read what Su Yun says about how the commune is organised. Then draw and complete a table like the one below, allowing more space for your answers.

	Size	Work
Production team		
Brigade		
Commune		

❶ In the area in which you live, who is responsible for (a) farm work (if you live in the country), (b) water supply, (c) tree planting, (d) road building, (e) electricity, (g) education and (h) health care?

At the commune headquarters, a group of workers discuss the changes the commune has brought.

I know we get paid each week but it is the same whether we work hard or whether we are lazy.

Sometimes the party officials tell us to grow rice on land which is not suitable. We don't make such mistakes on our own private plots.

Each family has a plot to grow food for itself. I think we would grow more if all the land was divided into private plots.

The food is fairly shared out now; we get a food ration each week as well as some cash.

At one time the government said we must concentrate on industry. The crops were neglected and a lot of people starved.

We generate our own electricity from the water that leaves the dam. Every house has electricity.

We have our own schools. All the children go to them. I never went to school. I had to help on the land.

We can repair our own machinery, make cement and bricks, make our own fertiliser. No wonder we can earn more money.

We have levelled off more land. It can be irrigated and drained properly and on the steep slopes, trees have been planted so the soil doesn't wash away.

The only people who like the communes are Communist Party officials who sit in an office all day.

❸ Decide which of the ten comments above are in favour of the commune and which are not. List them in what you think is their order of importance. (It would help if the comments were duplicated on card and cut up. You could work in groups.)

❹ Use the figures in the table on the right. Divide them into three groups:
■ Production expenses
■ Money put aside or paid in tax
■ Money distributed to members.
Work out what percentage of the money was given to each of the three groups.

How the money was divided in one year on a commune

Use of money	%
Production expenses (seed, fertiliser etc.)	30
Agricultural tax (paid to government)	7
Reserve fund (for new equipment)	6
Welfare fund (for those without a family to support them)	2
Reserve grain (for poor years)	5
Distributed to members	50
TOTAL	100

❺ Draw a pie chart to illustrate the three groups listed in question 4. To what extent do you think the commune plans for the future?

1980 onwards – the Responsibility System

Den Xiaoping

Mao Zedong died in 1976. The new leader of China was Deng Xiaoping (pronounced Show-ping). Gradually a new system began to replace the communes. Journalists report on the changes:

The Price of Profit

The amount of food grown has increased. Many farmers make a good profit. But who wants to clean out ditches and irrigation canals? Who is worried about their children being in school? There is no profit in it.

Not all peasants are well off. Some are poor and work for the richer ones. The land is being worked in separate plots again. The benefits of the commune are being lost. We are killing the chicken to get the eggs.

MORE OF EVERYTHING

In 1982, I visited the Evergreen People's Commune, just outside Beijing. What a change from the endless fields of wheat I saw on my last visit! Acres of cabbage were being cut for sale in the city. Tomatoes were being tended in large plastic greenhouses and crops of onions, carrots, peppers and spinach were growing in great quantities.

The people seemed better off too – 80% of the families on the commune have a TV, 70% have electric fans to cool their houses in the heat of summer. Fridges and tape recorders are common. They were only found in hotels a few years ago.

TURNING OVER A NEW LEAF

When the tea picking by the Shuang Feng Tea Brigade was organised by the commune, people used to wait until they were told what to pick. Then they picked the large leaves because it was easier.

But small leaves make a better type of tea which sells for a higher price. As the tea pickers can now keep some of the profit from the tea, they pick small leaves. They do this even though they have to pick leaves up to 30 times a year instead of six or seven.

In 1978 families earned about £250 a year. In 1986 this had risen to over £1,000 a year. In addition they can earn money working in a factory in a nearby town.

Since 1980, families in the countryside have not had to do work organised by the commune. They can contract to work an area of land and use it like their own private plot. For this they have to pay some money to local government and sell them a fixed amount of grain as well as pay taxes. Anything they grow or earn above this they can keep for themselves.

SMALLER FAMILIES

FIRST COME, FIRST SERVED

PLANNING — A BASIS — NATIONAL POLICY OF CHINA

China began a birth control campaign in 1980 with the slogan **ONE CHILD IS GOOD**.

Ten million Chinese are born each year and 62% of the population is under 32 years of age. The government is concerned about this.

Since the start of the campaign over ten million couples have signed a pledge to limit the size of their family to a single child. Signing the pledge brings certain advantages.

In Shanghai, couples who marry late get more time off for their honeymoon. Also the women get extra maternity leave and the family receive better housing. Eventually they will receive an increased retirement pension. Any couple that break their pledge have to pay back maternity, childcare and medical expenses.

Each area in China is given a yearly quota of births. Couples have to ask permission from local authorities before they can have children. In some areas it is very difficult to get permission for a second child and abortions are strongly encouraged if women become pregnant after their first child.

In Sechuan, the province of China with the highest population, the birth rate has been cut by a third. To achieve this a system was introduced in rural areas where extra children lost their share of farmland. Those with a single child receive a larger grain ration and other benefits.

However, in rural areas old traditions die hard and the tradition is to have as many children as possible. Many country-dwellers claim that officials have no business telling them how many children they can have. They say that, as long as they meet their production quotas they can choose how many children they have ... and many families are ignoring the government policy.

Work in pairs to answer questions 1 to 3. You will need to refer to the articles opposite.

❶ ⓐ How is the Responsibility system different from the Commune system?
ⓑ What effect has the change had on the Shuang Feng Tea Brigade described in 'Turning over a New Leaf'?

❷ Look at 'More of Everything'. Explain how there have been differences in:
ⓐ land use and
ⓑ the standard of living of the people.

❸ Suggest why the better living standards may not last long.

❹ Read the article 'First come, First served'.
ⓐ Why is a 'One Child' campaign necessary?
ⓑ How do the authorities try to enforce it?
ⓒ Write a play, short story or poem based on a Chinese couple trying to decide whether to have a second child.

❺ China is trying to feed a billion people. Over the years it has used different systems to do so. Would you prefer the Responsibility system or the Commune system? Explain fully the reasons for your choice.

LEARNING OBJECTIVES CHECKLIST

It is intended that the learning objectives summarized in these matrices should be used as the basis for assessment (see Teacher Resources). The content of the book provides a foundation for the development of language, numerical and oral skills.

UNIT CONTENT – CROSS CURRICULAR DIMENSIONS		THE FUTURE OF ANTARCTICA: political, aesthetic, scientific	SPARE THOSE TREES: economic, political	A CHANGE OF SCENE: historical, economic, aesthetic
UNDERSTANDING CONCEPTS	people/environment relationships	●	●	●
	systems	●	●	
	conservation	●	●	●
	change	●	●	●
	conflict	●	●	
	planning	●		●
	inequality - class/race		●	●
	political power distribution	●	●	
	relative location			●
	migration			●
	concentration/dispersal			●
	networks			●
	behaviourism			●
	scale/distance	●	●	●
	similarity/difference			
	prediction	●	●	●
	economic development	●	●	
MASTERING SKILLS AND TECHNIQUES — COLLECTING INFORMATION:	through fieldwork			
	from secondary sources	●		●
COMMUNICATING INFORMATION:	line graph			
	divided bar graph	●	●	
	bar graph			
	circular/flow diagram			
	creative writing	●		
	art/design work			●
	statistical techniques			●
INTERPRETING INFORMATION:	line graph		●	
	divided bar graph			
	bar graph		●	
	pie graph			
	age/sex pyramid			●
	pictorial graph			
	cross section/contours	●		
	ground level photos	●	●	●
	oblique air photos			●
	use of atlas	●	●	●
	reflective use of text	●	●	●
	numerical data		●	
	cartoons			
	documentary evidence			●
	diagrams/landscape sketches	●	●	
	large scale maps			●
	sketch maps/other maps/plans	●		●
EVALUATING:	role play/games/simulations			
	decision-making exercises	●		●
	group/pair discussion	●	●	●
SYNTHESIS:	research/investigation	●		
	empathising	●		
CLARIFYING VALUES AND ATTITUDES ABOUT	inequalities within society			●
	individual's quality of life		●	●
	justice/fairness		●	
	quality of environment	●	●	●
	need to accommodate/question change	●	●	●
	how change affects individuals		●	●
	responsibility to society/future generations	●	●	
	need to consider a range of opinions	●	●	

A NEW BOMBAY:
economic, political

INDUSTRIAL GROWTH AND CHANGE:
historical, economic, aesthetic

COMING AND GOING:
economic, aesthetic

DO WE STAY OR GO?
economic, scientific

SHOULD THE DESERT BLOOM?
economic, aesthetic

SRI LANKA – ISLAND OF DREAMS?
historical, economic, political

PEOPLE AND SPACE IN SOUTH AFRICA:
historic, economic, political

FEEDING A BILLION PEOPLE?:
historical, economic, political

AMENITIES: services which are provided for people who live in an area e.g. schools, shops, garages, village hall, community centre etc.

AQUEDUCTS: artificial channels for carrying water from one area to another.

BIRTH RATE: the number of babies born in a year for every thousand people in the population.

BLAST FURNACE: a large furnace over 25 metres high, used to melt iron ore to produce iron. Iron ore, limestone and coke are placed in the top of the furnace and a blast of hot air causes them to burn fiercely until the iron melts from the rock and is taken from the bottom of the furnace.

BUDDHIST: a Buddhist is a member of a religious group most usually found in south and east Asia.

BY-PRODUCTS: what is left over after something is made e.g. chemicals following the refining of oil. Some by-products can be treated to make other products.

COAL SEAMS: layers of coal beneath the earth's surface.

COMMERCIAL: used to describe the activity of trading or buying and selling goods.

CONGESTION: usually concerned with transport when there is so much traffic that it stops or slows down the movement.

CONSERVATION: is protecting, preserving and carefully managing natural resources. In the countryside this means protecting the natural landscape and managing farms to cause least damage to it.

CONTINENT: one of six large areas of land which make up the world. They are Africa, North America, South America, Antarctica, Asia and Europe.

DEATH RATE: the number of people who die in a year for every thousand people in the population.

DELTA: an area of flat land at the mouth of a river which extends out into the sea. (It takes its name from the Greek word for a letter D.) Deltas are formed by mud and silt brought down by rivers.

DENSITY: the number of objects in a certain area e.g. the number of people or houses in a square kilometre. A low population density would mean that there were very few people in an area.

DISCRIMINATION: making clear the differences between two people or groups and favouring one rather than the other.

DRIFT: very fine fallen snow which is blown by strong winds, making it difficult to see very far. Snow often collects to form **snow drifts** which are patches of deeper snow.

EMIGRATE: to leave one country or region to settle in another.

ENVIRONMENT: a person's surroundings. This may refer to the room they are in or the surroundings in a town or in the countryside. The word has particularly come to be used by people when speaking of the need to provide pleasant surroundings or protect an attractive environment for all to enjoy.

EXPLOIT: to make use of someone or something for your own gain.

FACILITIES: services which are provided for people such as car parks, toilets, cafés, or information centres in a park.

FERMENTING: the way in which some food and drink products are left to undergo a chemical change which alter their appearance and taste. Grape juice is fermented in order to make wine.

FINISHED PRODUCTS: those articles, which have been made by a factory, in their finished form.

FOSSIL: a plant, animal or insect which lived and died millions of years ago, found in some rocks. It may be in the form of a stone or it may leave a print in the earth.

GEOLOGIST: a person who studies rocks and how they are made.

GLACIER(S): a mass of ice made of hard packed snow which collects in large hollows on mountains. Glaciers move slowly down river valleys making them wider and deeper. They can be over 50 kilometres long, 5 kilometres wide and 1000 metres deep.

HINDUS: people who follow the religion of Hinduism. Hindus are found mainly in India.

HYDROELECTRIC: making electricity by using water power.

ICE SHEET: ice hundreds of metres thick covering a large area and formed from the build up of snowfall. Ice sheets cover much of Antarctica and the Arctic and some high mountain areas. In Antarctica the ice sheet is moving steadily outwards from the Pole and floating out into the sea. **Icebergs** are large chunks of ice that have broken off and floated away from the edge of the ice sheet.

IRRIGATE: to water crops artificially because the rainfall is too low when the crops need water.

MALNUTRITION: poor health caused by a poorly balanced diet. As a result, people become weak and catch diseases easily.

MANIOC: a type of bush which grows in the tropics. Its roots can be boiled to provide food. It is sometimes called cassava and provides us with tapioca.

MARKET(S): a place where goods are sold which may be a town, a country or part of a country.

MEAN ANNUAL SURFACE TEMPERATURE: an average of the yearly temperature taken at ground level.

MERIDIAN: an imaginary line round the earth which passes through the north and south Poles and is used by nagivators.

METEOROLOGIST: a person who studies the weather.

MIGRANTS: people who move from one country or area to another in order to live and work.

MIGRATE: to go from one place to settle in another.

MINERALS: found in rock. They may be mined or quarried and either melted down, like iron and copper to make metal, or used as a source of power such as coal and oil.

MULTINATIONAL: a very large company, with factories in many different countries, often making and selling a range of products.

NATIONALISATION: the owning and running of businesses by the State or country in which they are found.

NATURAL DISASTER(S): a great force of nature which causes large loss of life or damage to property or landscape. Volcanoes, earthquakes, storms and floods are examples.

NATURAL INCREASE: the increase in population as a result of more babies being born than people dying.

NATURALIST: a person who studies animals and plants.

NETWORK: the links between a number of places (or routes) such as roads and railways.

ORE: a rock containing minerals which may be mined or quarried and then melted down in a furnace to make metal, for example, **iron ore**, copper ore and tin ore.

ORNITHOLOGIST: a person who studies birds.

OVERPRODUCTION: producing too much of a product so that there is so much it is difficult to sell it all.

OZONE LAYER: a layer high in the atmosphere which consists of ozone, a form of oxygen, which helps to protect us from the harmful effects of the sun's rays.

POLDER(S): an area of low lying land which has been reclaimed from a sea, lake or river. This is done by building a dyke (bank) around the area and pumping the water out.

PROTEIN: an important part of food which provides the body with building materials. It is found mainly in animal products like milk, cheese, meat and fish.

QUARRIED: a quarry is a large pit dug to obtain a mineral from the ground. Rocks and ores are quarried.

RACIST: a person or a government can be racist. This means that they believe that people of other races are inferior to them. Also see entry for DISCRIMINATION.

RAW MATERIALS: those items from which more complex items are made e.g. jam is made from fruit and sugar: fruit and sugar are the raw materials. Steel is made using coal, iron and limestone: coal, iron and limestone are the raw materials.

RECREATION: anything people do in their spare time to enjoy themselves.

RENOVATE(D): to repair a house or housing area of a city and improve its condition.

REPATRIATION: people are returned to their homeland from the country in which they have been living.

RESOURCES: land, property, minerals or people which can be used to earn income. Coal, iron ore, forests and skilled workers are all resources.

SILT: fine particles which have been worn away from rock and deposited by a river.

SITE(S): ground on which a building or town stands or is to stand or be located.

SUBURBS: areas of housing around the outer edge of towns or cities.

TERRACED: fields on steep hillsides are terraced to provide flat growing areas for crops.

TROPICAL: the areas of the world which are close to the Equator, between the Tropic of Cancer and the Tropic of Capricorn.

UNITED NATIONS: an international organisation based in New York, to which most countries of the world belong.

ACKNOWLEDGEMENTS

Copyright © 1987 Richard Clammer, Brian Greasley, Trevor Higginbottom, Peter McLeod, Richard Nicholls

ISBN 0 00 326602 8

Published by Collins Educational, 8 Grafton Street, London W1X 3LA

First published 1987
Reprinted 1988 (Twice)

Design and artwork by Malcolm Porter
Illustrations by Chris Hill and Ann Baum
Cartoons by Peter Schrank
Cover photograph by Sally and Richard Greenhill
Picture research by Veneta Bullen

Typeset by Swanston Graphics, Derby
Printed and bound by Wing King Tong, Hong Kong

Photographs The publisher would like to thank the following for permission to reproduce photographs:

Aerophoto-Schiphol B.V. 18, 21, 25; Bryan and Cherry Alexander 3, 88b; Patrick Bailey 82br; Richard Baker 68; Tom Bean 59tr, 62br; British Antarctic Survey 2, 4b, 5b, 5t, 6; Central Arizona Project/Bureau of Reclamation 59tl, 60; Prodeepta Das 53, 56tl; DVC/BL Fodis 22b, 24; Earthscape 59bl, 62c; Paul Forster 15t, 82tl; Adam Ginalski 62tl; Richard and Sally Greenhill 58, 66t, 69, 82bl, 85, 88c, 89; The Guardian 71; Robert Harding Associates 57t, 62tr, 66b; Hutchinson Library 12r, 12l, 13, 15b, 19, 22t, 26, 27, 28, 29, 31l, 34, 45, 49, 54l, 57b, 59br, 72, 74b, 77r, 82tr, 86t, 86c; International Defence & Aid Fund 76; Jim Lewis/University of Durham 42, 48; Link, Ben Edwards 26tr; Orde Eliason 74c, 75, 79; The Mansell Collection 78; Nancy Durrell McKenna 80; National Film Archives 31r; Natural History Photo Library 4t, 6c; NOAA/Science Photo Library 51; Network/Eric Miller/Afrapix 81; Panos Pictures 17; Renault 46t; Silkcut Travel/Graham Phillips 11; South African Tourist Board 77r; South American Pictures/Tony Morrison 15c; Frank Spooner Pictures 46, 50, 56bl, 73, 74t, 78t; Tass 34, 35, 37, 39, 40; John Topham Picture Library 8; Penny Tweedie 54r; VVV Flevoland 24.

t=top, b=bottom, c=centre, l=left, r=right.